request.response.reaction

First published in Australia in 2002 by
The Images Publishing Group Pty Ltd
ABN 89 059 734 431
6 Bastow Place, Mulgrave, Victoria, 3170, Australia
Telephone: +61 3 9561 5544 Facsimile: +61 3 9561 4860
Email: books@images.com.au
Website: www.imagespublishinggroup.com

Copyright © The Images Publishing Group Pty Ltd
The Images Publishing Group Reference Number: 474

National Library of Australia
Cataloguing-in-Publication data

Crafti, Stephen
Request.Response.Reaction. The designers of Australia & New Zealand

Includes index.
ISBN: 1 876907 51 7

1. Artists – Australia. 2. Artists – New Zealand. 3. Art, Australian. 4. Art, New Zealand. 5. Art, modern 20th century. 6. Design – Australia. 7. Design – New Zealand. I. Title. II. Title : Request, response, reaction

709.9

Co-ordinating Editor: Joe Boschetti
Designed by The Graphic Image Studio Pty Ltd, Mulgrave, Australia
Film by Mission Productions Limited, Hong Kong
Printed by Sing Cheong Printing Co. Ltd. Hong Kong

IMAGES has included on its website a page for special notices in relation to this and our other publications. Please visit this site: www.imagespublishinggroup.com

request
.respon
se.reac
tion

CONTENTS

jewellery:

Jewellery is traditionally valued for the number of carats within the stones. Whether made of gold or silver, the cluster of diamonds or rubies created the impression. However, with the likes of jewellers such as Susan Cohn, Mari Funaki, Marian Hosking, Warwick Freeman, Dinosaur Designs and Alan Preston, mentioning carats and clusters is of little relevance.

Instead of the brilliant shimmer of diamonds, it is the ideas behind each piece that becomes the object's most important jewel. Whether the piece is made of plastic, resin or silver, the forms can be unravelled to tell their own stories.

ceramics, glass and metal:

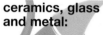

From blasting to firing, designers in these mediums continue to explore their boundaries. Simple household objects are the source of inspiration for one designer, while another sees forms as she lies awake at night. The designs sometimes evoke the past while clearly pointing to the future. The objects demand to be touched as much as admired. Irrespective of the process, the objects often take on a hand-crafted feel. Working in their own medium, Stephane P. Rondel, Simon Lloyd, Robert Foster, Maureen Williams and Robert Knottenbelt display the extraordinary depth of their craft.

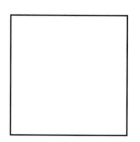

sculpture:

You need to walk around them and examine them from every angle. The subject might be figurative, or alternatively speak of the native landscape. The sculpture may be meticulously carved or welded together. The sculptors featured in this book, Geoffrey Bartlett, Peter D Cole, Inge King, Augustine Dall'Ava and Robert Bridgewater work on different scales and in a variety of materials. However, the presence of each work is overwhelming when encountered either in the landscape or within a building. Even when a sculpture finds its way to the top of a city apartment building, the anticipation is part of the presentation.

furniture:

Furniture has always been a challenge for Australian and New Zealand designers. With a relatively short history of furniture design, finding the right manufacturers to produce relatively small volumes has always been a problem. Similarly, Australian retailers tend to source their requirements from overseas suppliers. However, with the wealth of talent that has started to emerge over the last few decades, the focus of the industry is now closer to home.

Furniture designed by Marc Newson, Caroline Casey, Map, Join, Humphrey Ikin, David Trubridge, Tim Miller or Schamburg & Alvisse, is being shown in galleries as well as furniture showrooms. From the iconic to the highly functional, each piece has been resolved to the *nth-degree*. Made of aluminium or the more traditional timbers, the designs continue to challenge established parameters.

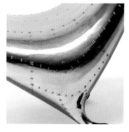

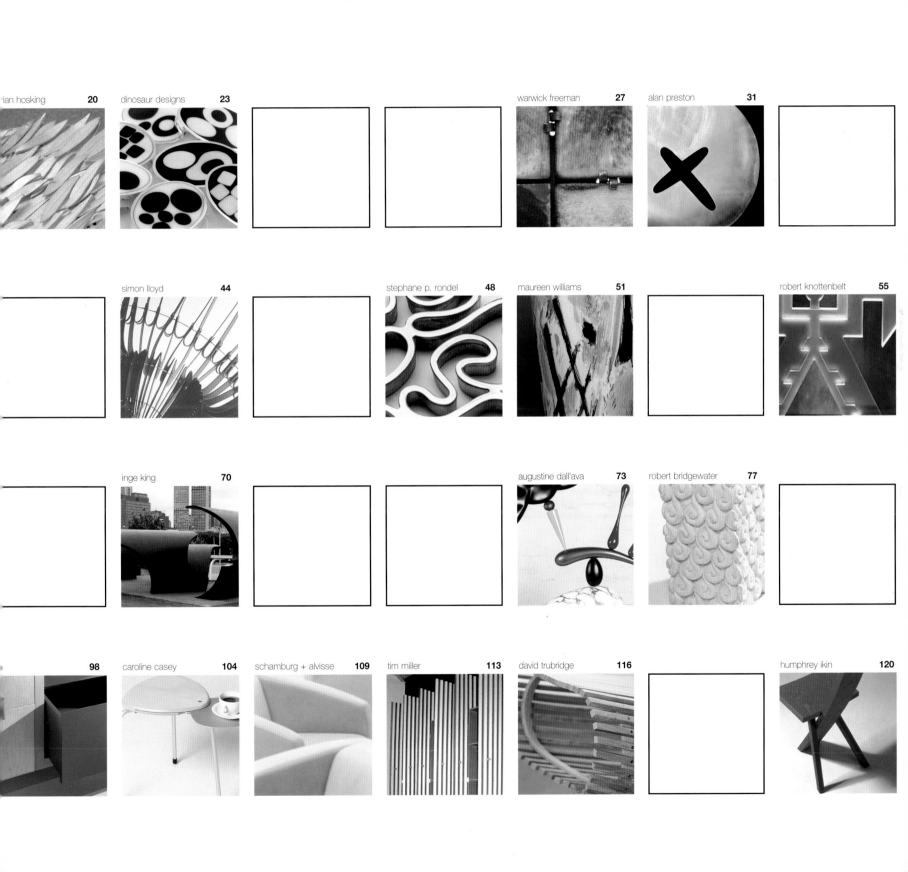

lighting:

The glamour and the glitz of the 1980s was all the more brilliant as a result of the small and infinite number of halogen lights that dotted ceilings throughout Australia and New Zealand. With the flick of one switch the sharp lighting was amplified by reflecting off substantial marble surfaces. Replacing the halogen globes was as frustrating as keeping these surfaces in pristine condition. When the brilliant 1980s lost their shine, there began a gradual move to more subtle lighting and a new lighting culture emerged.

In the 1990s it was the European labels that stole the spotlights. The European names were a dominant force in designer lighting. However, the ingenuity of Australian and New Zealand designers has also had its chance to shine. As mentioned by Ross Madden, who operates the R.G. Madden designer homewares stores in Australia, 'A light shouldn't be sold on the basis of where it was made. It should be sold because it's well resolved and takes the level of design up another notch'. The lights of Denis Smitka, Ism Objects, Marc Pascal and Schamburg & Alvisse, best exemplify this ideal, creating new lighting forms in the process.

graphic design:

Graphic design incorporates numerous design fields. It could be a label on a shelf, or a sign to help us find our way through a building. Whatever the form, the images have been finely manipulated to create a clear, often lingering message.

Given the strength and importance of graphic design, it is an area of design that is rarely profiled. We see the signs, we see the images and we appreciate the humour at times. However, it is often taken for granted as something that should just be there, like the pavements in our streets. When you look at the work of some leading graphic designers – Garry Emery Design, Brian Sadgrove, Ken Cato, Cornwell Design, Fabio Ongarato, Storm Image and Asprey di Donato – from the graphically simple to the confronting, the styles are as varied as the practices themselves.

photography:

Photographers John Gollings, Andrew Curtis, Peter Hyatt, Daniel MacDougall, Greg Barrett and Trevor Mein show with their images the power of the camera lens. During the day, an industrial machine serves as a functional device. However, at night through the photographer's eye, the same machine explodes with animation. A building is transformed from bricks and mortar into a majestic piece of sculpture. A series of objects, carefully arranged, appears as a series of family portraits. Whether the images are disturbing or simply uplifting, the photographer's eye creates a new angle for the observer.

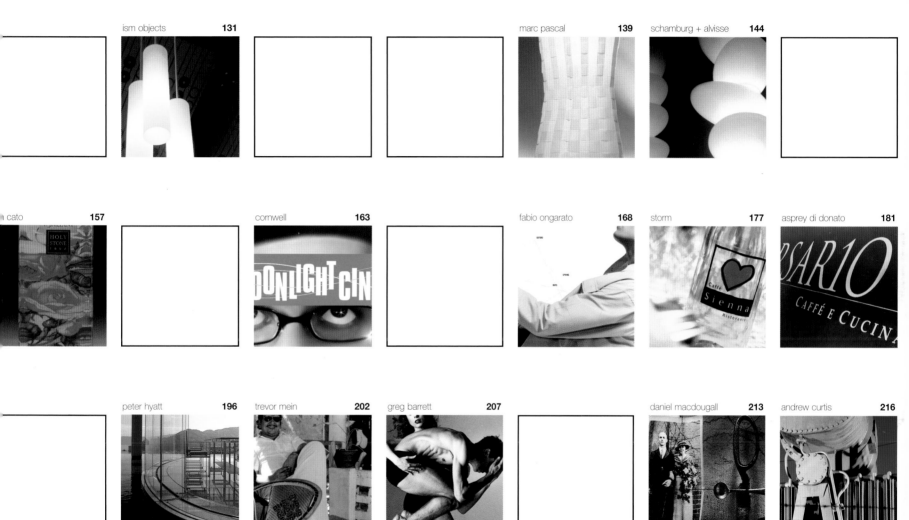

8

Given the population size of Australia and New Zealand, there is an extraordinary range of talent residing within these countries. Instead of looking towards Europe for their inspiration, the designers featured in this book speak their own language and of the influences closer to home.

The artists and the design fields covered in this book are diverse, but there are a number of important links. Finding out how someone approaches their work has always fascinated me. The approach might be an idea that comes in the night and is quickly sketched out first thing in the morning. Others prefer the trial-and-error method, continually experimenting with materials until the form takes shape. Whatever form the design takes, in two or three dimensions, each has a unique spirit that challenges many of the traditional approaches.

Whether the medium is jewellery, sculpture, furniture, ceramics, glass, metal, lighting, graphic design or photography, there is a sense of adventure with each project. A piece of jewellery is carefully unravelled to reveal a story, so too the graphic image, which clearly sends out its message. The sculpture, which stops us in our tracks, asks as many questions as it answers.

Each designer in this book could form the basis of a separate story. The purpose of this book is to tell their stories in their words and through their work. The determination of these designers, combined with talent, will hopefully stimulate and inspire us all.

Stephen Crafti

jewellery

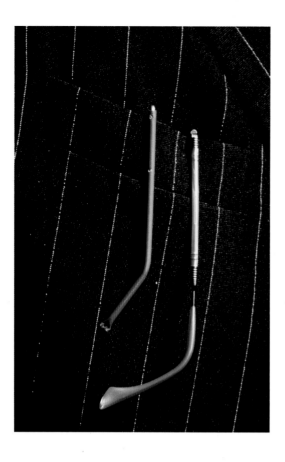

SUSAN COHN - PURE GOLD

After training and working in graphic design for a number of years, Susan Cohn wanted to go beyond two-dimensional design. Following a brief stint in fashion in the 1970s, the idea of jewellery kept resurfacing. The conversations, which headed towards jewellery, came at a time when plastics were starting to appear overseas. At the gold and silversmithing course at RMIT, Cohn's second-year project was a plastic hair comb that was based on the Pompidou Centre. 'I had to talk my way into Ciba Geigy, who are plastic and adhesive specialists in Melbourne. The plastic had to be flexible and the electric blue colour came as a result of much trial and error,' Cohn says.

Soon after graduation, Cohn set up Workshop 3000 (Melbourne's postcode) with jeweller Marian Hosking, bringing in the lathes, the presses and the specialist machinery. The large doughnut-shaped bracelets which were made of aluminium, formed part of Cohn's early work and still form an important part of her collection, though the form and material continue to evolve.

Cohn's condom series of pendants and holders has recently been taken up by Alessi. The dragonfly pendant (the more elaborate of the pendants) conceals a condom holder and takes the idea of protection to a higher level. The Lalique-inspired pendant is composed of sunglasses and wind sockets. 'It dances around your genitals and will bite the fingers off someone you don't want near you. However, it will deliver a condom for those who do. It's about the power to make a choice,' Cohn says.

Cohn has been working on possible 'body sites' for jewellery since the early 1990s. 'Simple brooches can be used on one's face to iron out the ageing defects such as sagging chins'. The cosmetic manipulations not only eliminate the surgeon's knife, but highlight areas that are often considered unattractive. For an adolescent child, self conscious of braces, with a piece of Cohn's jewellery enmeshed in the wires, the notion of braces takes on a new meaning.

While Cohn's jewellery continues to be applauded on the world stage, she says that her greatest pleasure comes from seeing someone who has bought a piece of her work which then becomes part of their identity. 'That beats having designs sitting on a museum shelf'.

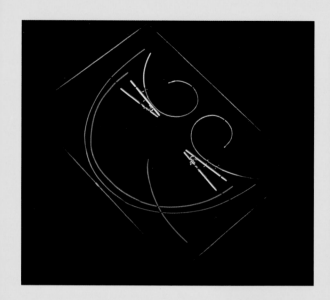
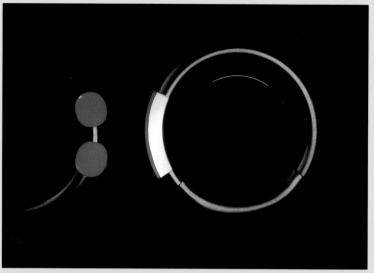

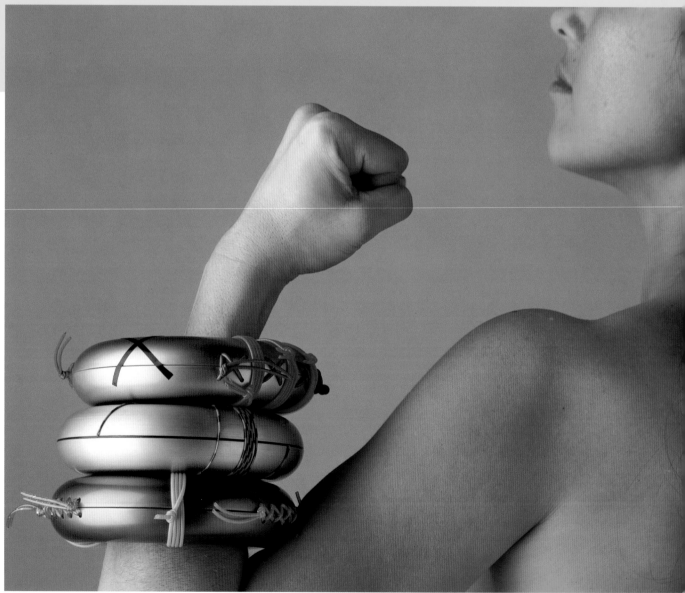

For Mari Funaki, designing jewellery was not an immediate career decision. Growing up on a farm in Matsue, Japan, there were few artistic distractions. While Funaki's parents were running the farm, it was her auntie who introduced her to drawing and painting. 'I still remember her wonderful watercolours,' Funaki says. Like most children who are fascinated by insects, Funaki spent hours examining the structure of these creatures. 'I love the detail and all the hidden spaces behind the wings,' she says.

Funaki's jewellery, which has a strong architectural feel, captures the fine details and spatial qualities of the container. With childhood memories of insects, such as grass-hoppers, her container-like jewellery takes on the sinuous lines of the insect. A 22-carat gold ring, for example, recalls the form of an insect's wings, with a series of layers carefully wound around one's finger. The mild steel metal containers, which are oxidised to create a rich black patina, express Funaki's desire to create work that has a pure quality with an inner strength. While the smaller containers can be attached to the edge of a jacket, others are best appreciated on a shelf. Resembling extraordinary architectural models, the objects could well be translated into a future 'container for people'.

MARI FUNAKI – FINELY ASSEMBLED

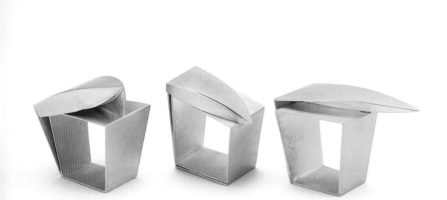

'Many people relate my work to Japanese paper origami perhaps because of my nationality, the use of paper-thin metal and the animate quality in my work. However, my work is based on a method of cutting, rather than folding. My pieces are assembled or constructed together by many sheets of metal, like constructing a building, in rather an intuitive way,' she says. As the work unfolds, so do the spatial relationships within each piece.

Whether Funaki's jewellery is influenced by insects or the architectural lines around her, there's a strong emotive quality with each piece. As Funaki says, 'My designs begin as two-dimensional drawings. However, I work intuitively. There's not a plan which is systematically executed. It's important that the work has its own voice'.

MARIAN HOSKING - CAPTURING THE LIGHT

Jeweller and Silversmith Marian Hosking finds inspiration from the Australian bush. Hosking's fine brooches, chains, bracelets and containers are all exquisitely detailed in silver using the drill and jeweller's saw. For Hosking, who has been designing for 30 years, silver has been the preferred medium.

'Silver has a soft white appearance. It highlights and shifts shadows and captures the intense light of the Australian bush,' says Hosking. The designs, which depict plants and birds, also reveal the human aspect of the process with the small marks deliberately left by the designer. Hosking, who is the studio co-ordinator of Metals and Jewellery in the Faculty of Art and Design at Monash University in Melbourne, still finds the time to exhibit her work around the country. Even placed under a microscope, Hosking's designs reveal an extraordinary attention to detail.

Light and pattern are two elements that continually inform Hosking's designs. 'Since the early 1970s I have sought to convey a sense of place in much of my work.

Two aspects particularly interest me, light and the difference between seemingly alike elements. The pieces I have been making recently encapsulate light and its subtle shifts across the surfaces,' she says. Using a fine jeweller's saw, the many cut lines which create negative spaces appear to shift as the viewer or object moves in relation to the light source. 'The shapes which break up the surface appear to jostle for space. At times they appear to devour it. The pieces rely on repetition and recognition, rhythmic shifts and eddies, subtle variations and tensions'.

Since the early 1990s, Hosking has also been making a series of boxes. From the hay shed to the suburban house, there is a continual exploration of light and shadow. The saw-pierced lines, which create a sense of depth to each box take on the appearance of crosshatching in a freehand drawing. While the lines of the bales stacked neatly in Hosking's *Hay Shed* are confined under the shed's roofline, the leaves on her brooches spill over the edges.

'It's a consciously feminine exploration of metalwork that constitutes a break from the traditional maleness that has dominated the craft since its ancient beginnings in weapon making,' Hosking says. The exploration, which leads to the creation of delicate patterns, could almost be mistaken for the finest embroidery.

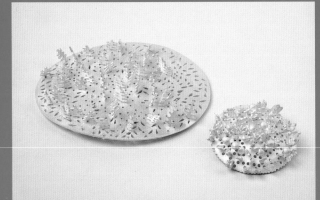

Soon after graduating from art school in 1985, designers Louise Olsen, Stephen Ormandy and Liane Rossler formed Dinosaur Designs. More than 15 years later, the trio have clearly cemented a place for themselves among Australia's leading designers. With retail outlets across Australia and supplying some of the world's finest retailers, including their first store in New York, Dinosaur Designs continues to gain momentum.

While the trio appear to work independently of slavish trends, they are acutely aware of market forces. As Ormandy says, 'Our first venture after graduating was printing fabric and sewing it into garments. We made jewellery out of fimo (like a modelling clay) to accessorise the clothing'. The jewellery became the most sought-after items and hence the direction taken by the team. Replacing the fimo with resin, this material has become synonymous with their designs. Even though each design is made in multiples, each piece is still handmade and sculpted individually. 'It's still quite a primitive form of production in comparison to mass-produced items. However, there's a human and tactile quality to each piece. The colours are all mixed by hand and each is unique,' Olsen says.

Sterling silver cufflinks illustrate the diversity of Dinosaur Designs. When men's cufflinks generally lean towards the conservative side, Dinosaur's graphic designs take the simple accessory to new heights. The resin takes on the appearance of glass, it appears more irregular. 'We enjoy that juxtaposition between the shapes, which are so primitive that you can see the dappled hallmarks on them, and the hi-tech materials we use. We want our jewellery and our homewares to be modern, but earthy and feel beautiful to touch,' Olsen says.

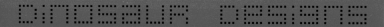 

DINOSAUR DESIGNS — A STRONG SIGNATURE

24

Whether the design is for their homewares range of products or for their jewellery, which includes earrings, bracelets and necklaces, there is often a strong theme running through the collections. 'We work in stories and themes, such as the sea, flowers, leaves and river rocks. The inspiration comes from nature's forms, tones and hues,' she says. The materials, like the ranges, are diverse, including sterling silver, wood, metal, glass and wax.

From jewellery to jewellery-like objects, there doesn't seem to be a time before Dinosaur Designs. Each new range has the Dinosaur hallmark; colour, vitality, clarity and a sense of vision that is rarely seen on such a scale.

WARWICK FREEMAN - JEWELLERY AT WORK

Self-taught jeweller Warwick Freeman has been making jewellery since the early 1970s. Instead of looking towards Europe for inspiration, Freeman looked to the Maori and Pacific Island cultures of New Zealand where he resides.

While each piece of Freeman's jewellery has an individual strength of its own, a number of pieces can be more fully appreciated in a group setting. The *Insignia* set, which includes a shield, a spot, a karaka leaf, an eye, a bird and a skull, acts as a narrative or complete sentence. 'When all the work is lined up it looks like you should make sense of it, it's all so familiar. It's a sign language, much like road signs and like the road signs, the pieces of jewellery are flat and two dimensional. However, unlike road signs, you can't be too sure what some of these pieces are telling you,' Freeman says. Freeman prefers us to make our own individual readings.

Some of Freeman's jewellery is a direct replication of their source. A key or a leaf is realised by drawing around the actual object. Other pieces, such as the *Flame* brooch, are interpreted as though the flame was frozen still for the artist to capture. Freeman's jewellery continually provides connections and adds new meaning to the simplest forms.

Flutter consists of a white heart, a black butterfly, a tongue and a kawakawa leaf which appear as varied as the materials used for each piece; scallop shell, basalt, jasper and greenstone. '*Flutter* is also slang for a small bet. I like this sort of word trail. I can move restlessly along it, a bit like a butterfly, settling only long enough to

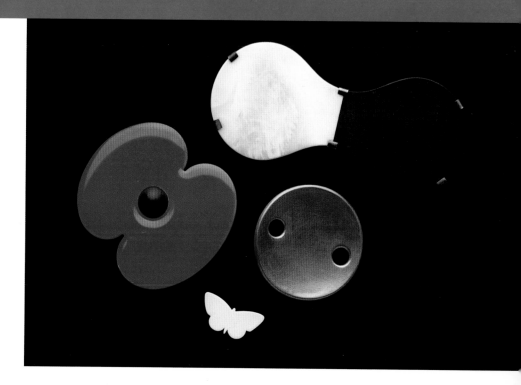

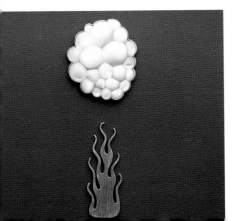

find a connection and then fluttering on,' Freeman says. When people add their interpretations to the collections, a complexity is added to the work. Freeman plays with the interpretations, like someone standing at a roulette table. 'Sometimes I win, sometimes I lose. Hey it's only jewellery, not much to bet with. You never know your luck, as the man says, *float like a butterfly …*'

Given the enormous recognition given to Freeman's work, there is an unusual sense of modesty. 'It's all old stuff. I just dress it up in new clothing, clothing cut from whatever materials I think will do the job'.

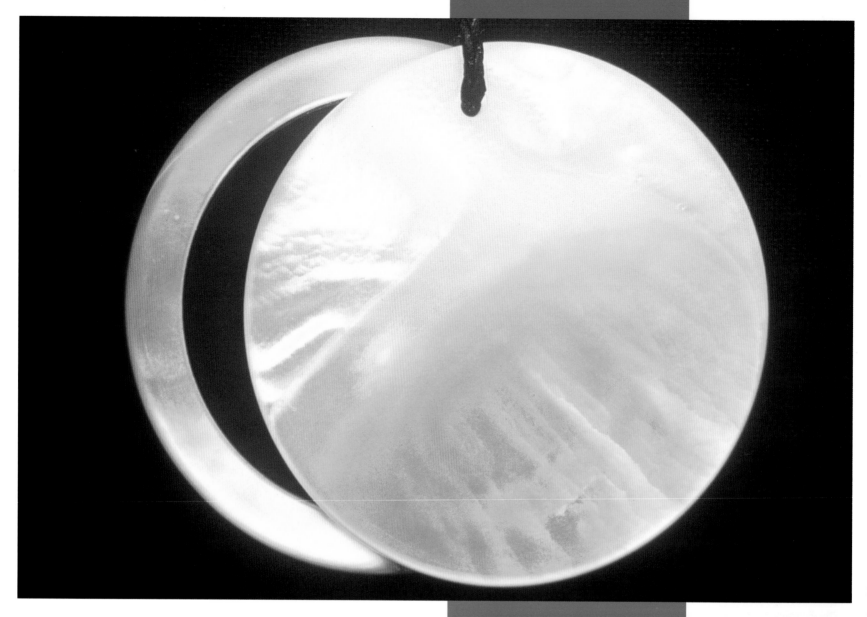

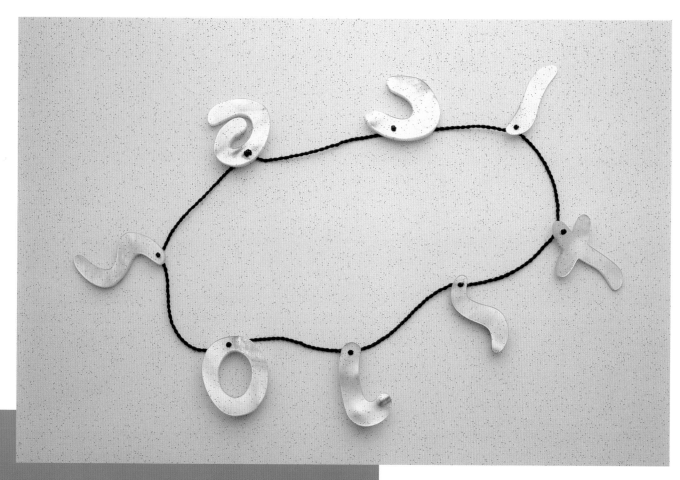

Focusing on his sense of place, jeweller Alan Preston is inspired by the Pacific region where he resides. 'I give thanks to the people of the Pacific and their ancestors. Their traditions, together with mine, are a source of ideas and inspiration for my comments about a new Oceania,' Preston says.

Using materials and techniques that belong to the place of Aotearoa, where Preston was born, his work clearly explores contemporary Pacific adornment. The materials of the ocean, which are finely woven into jewellery, are valued in the same way as the more traditional components of jewellery, such as gold and silver. The oyster and paua shell reveal the same richness as 18-carat gold. While the form of Preston's jewellery appears relatively uncomplicated at first glance, each piece is highly crafted and resolved. Preston's *Fish Necklace* for example, was designed so that each fish link is double hinged, and each fish takes on a fluidity of movement.

A strong theme to Preston's jewellery is his concern for conservation. Instead of using a material such as the oyster pearl shell, removing a shape and dispensing with the remains, the entire shell becomes the subject for a number of pieces. The *Four Pointer Brooch Breastplate* made of Blacklip oyster shell silver vau and the *Flower Breastplate* find their source from the same oyster shell. Removing the shape of the brooch from the breastplate shows the important nature of the negative image.

For Preston, the materials and Aotearoa and the Pacific region are the driving forces behind his jewellery. 'The work that I make is often generated by the previous pieces I have made. There is a certain degree of serendipity. Often I make work that I feel could have been made in the past or should have been made in the past given the materials and low-tech techniques available. So this is my version of Contemporary Pacific Adornment,' Preston says. For Preston, who has been exploring his craft since the late 1970s, the chains continue to find new links. 'Initially, there were some small chains made in the Anglo-Saxon tradition of seafarers who would make these sorts of things in bone or wood. The centre shapes from these chains inspired ideas for flower necklaces which refer back to Pacific motifs again. The large chain in turn generated a large lei from its middles, and so the chain continues'.

32

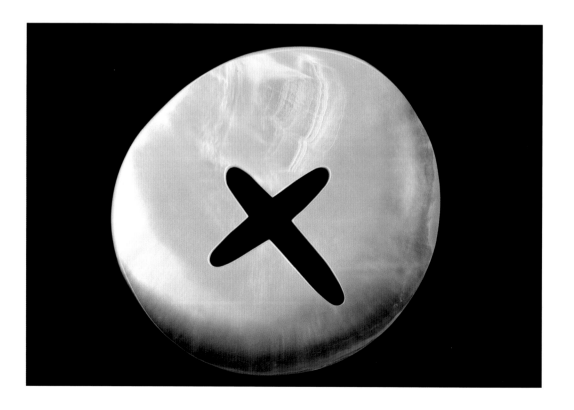

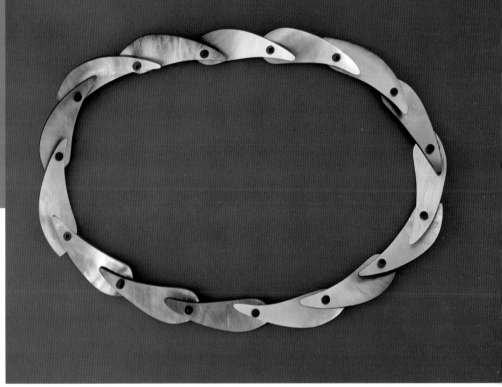

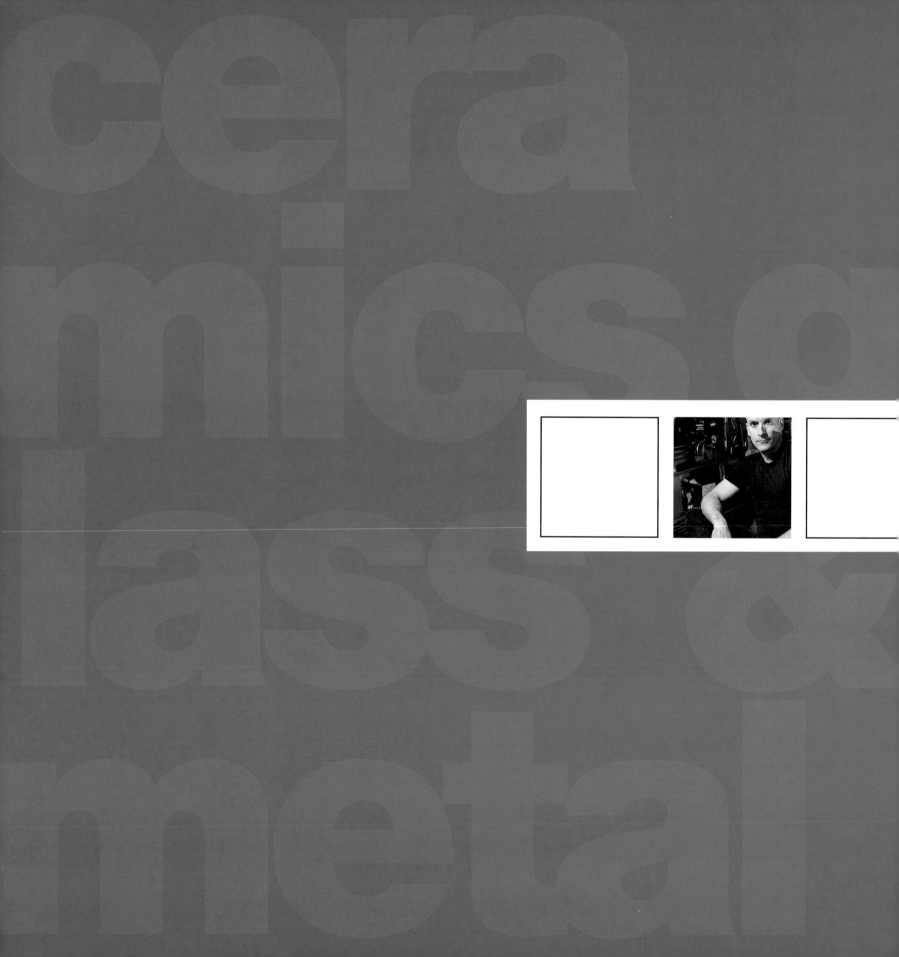

**ceramics, glass
and metal**

The *Fink Water Jug*, by designer Robert Foster of Fink and Co., is one of the few vibrant colours that are retained in many contemporary interiors. 'When the product entered the market in 1993, there was nothing like it,' says Foster. However, a number of years later, the jug still stands alone, both in terms of other products on the market, and usually from other utensils in the kitchen. The pressed aluminium and anodised jug with its powder-coated aluminium handle, makes it a natural choice for galleries and museums across Australia.

More recently the *Explosive Vase* has shared the limelight with the *Fink Water Jug*. 'The vase is made by using explosives. It gives the vase its organic and sensual shape. The way each vase is finished is unique. My objects take on a more high-tech handcrafted feel,' Foster says. For Foster, designing objects started at an early age, initially making jewellery as an adolescent in his father's shed. 'My father was a potter and an art school teacher which led me to play with ceramics from a young age. However, I was attracted to the qualities of metal, the ability to control it together with its versatility and precision,' Foster says. Continually experimenting with metal, Foster explores the endless surface treatments and processes of his craft. 'There's an ironic beauty of utilising volatile energy of high explosive to form an elegant and sensuous object. It has always fascinated me,' he says.

While a number of Fink and Co.'s products are designed in metal, others are cleverly juxtaposed with other materials, such as granite, glass, porcelain and plastics. The *Blink Lamp*, which is a small table or bedside lamp, includes a perforated brass head with a porcelain shade. The satin

nickel-plated stem not only supports the shade, but doubles as the light switch. The porcelain shade, which is covered with perforated brass, appears almost helmet-like. 'With many of our designs, there's a strong organic feel. *The Blink* could be compared to a flower,' Foster says. Whether the object is a vase or a jug, each piece has an energy of its own.

As each new product is released, the bar is raised. While each new design appears effortless, Foster is mindful of the research and development behind each design. 'I would say that my work is an evolving process of continual discovery. It doesn't happen spontaneously. Often it's trial and error, and simply experimenting with new technologies'.

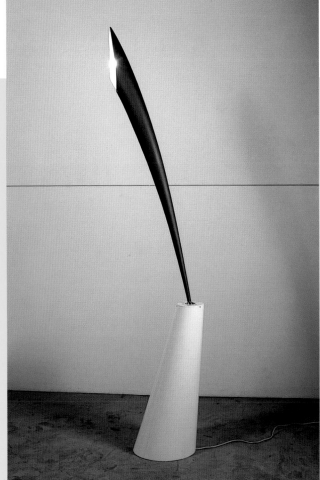

41

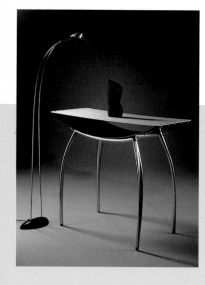

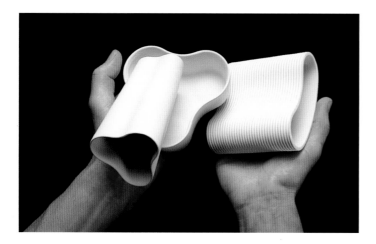

SIMON LLOYD – SURROUNDING IMAGES

Drawing on the past and redefining the present, designer Simon Lloyd finds inspiration from simple household objects and industrial relics. Lloyd, who trained at the High Wycombe Arts School in London, originally focused on furniture design before moving on to designing smaller household objects. Whether the object is made of steel or ceramic, each piece is meticulously crafted.

Lloyd's aluminium and iron candle holders were influenced by 19th-century cast iron warehouse columns. 'They recall the industrial revolution and the mechanisation of the time. The candle holders go through quite an intensive process. There's the pattern making in wood, then taken to the foundry and cast in sand boxes, before the metal is actually poured,' Lloyd says. Lloyd likens the production process to cooking. 'It's a matter of assembling all the ingredients. The results are there before you really start'. One cooking ingredient to influence Lloyd's work is the simple capsicum. The *Shell* vases have three-pronged highly glossed inner cores. In contrast to their gloss-white interiors, the exterior finishes are designed in matt, in subtle tones of chartreuse, ochre, charcoal and black.

When it came to designing the *Lighthouse*, made of clear glazed earthenware, Lloyd recalled the gas fire which he used to see while visiting the dentist as a child. 'Ideas might be dormant for years, but somehow manage to be triggered at a much later date,' he says. The exquisite comb-like lights with their dish-shaped tops can be used with essential oils to create a fragrance in a room. 'The conceptual idea is probably the most exciting part of the product's development and some household objects can appear in front of me a number of times before I take the cue'.

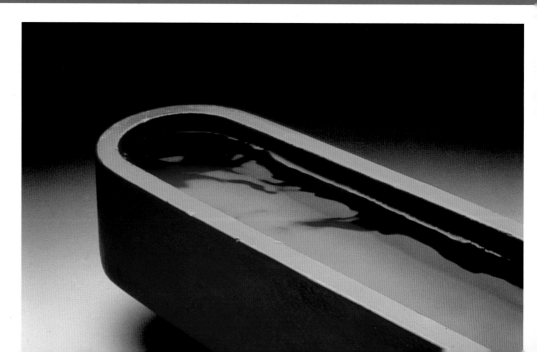

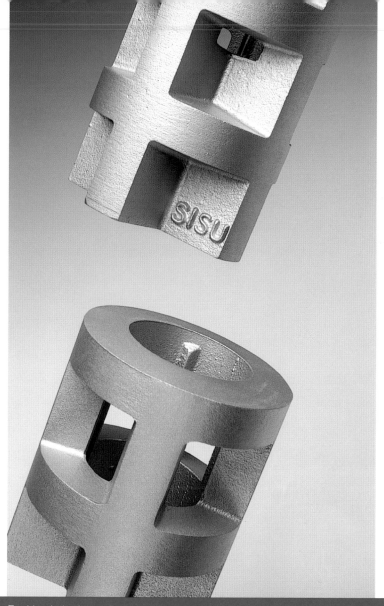

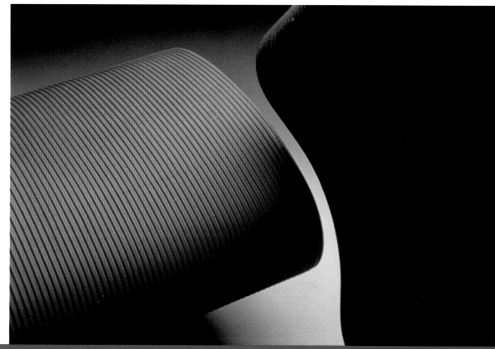

For Lloyd, the immediate environment and the surroundings during his formative years in England play an important role in his designs. 'Shapes and forms around my home and studio seem to act as memory triggers, which through constant recognition, form lasting images in the mind's eye. Without such triggers, boundaries into new fields wouldn't occur'. While Lloyd works in a number of separate media, he often integrates two different materials in the one design. Lloyd's silver cell bowl is inserted with a transparent acrylic layer. The bevelled edge of the acrylic creates an inner glow to the bowl. As Lloyd says, 'Exploring the use of materials and how these can be combined in the one object provide endless possibilities. The whole process can be so elusive that to see the idea finally becoming a reality is extremely satisfying'.

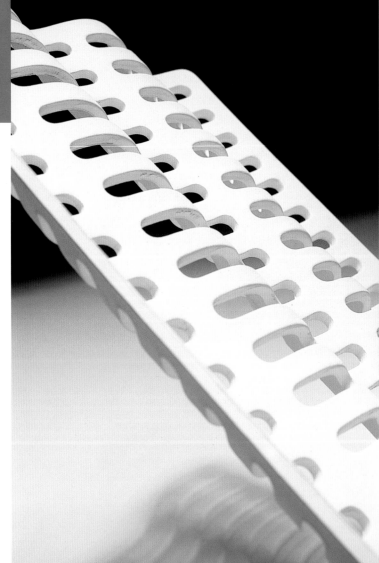

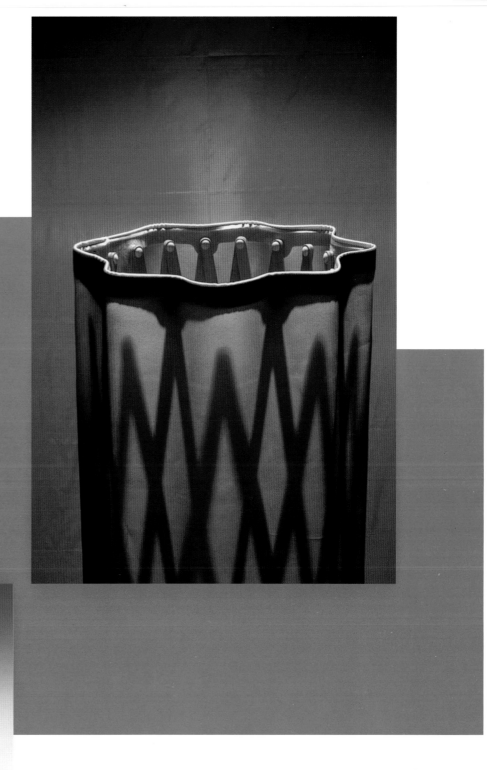

47

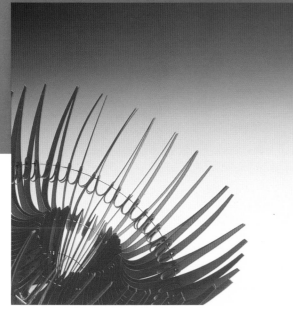

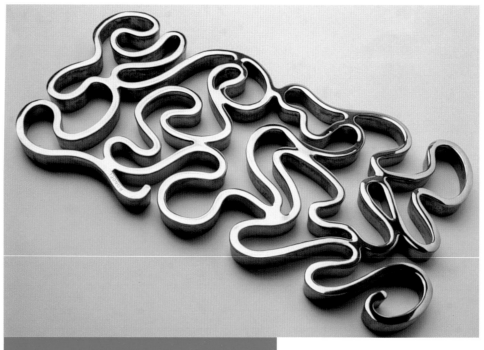

STEPHANE P. RONDEL – SINUOUS FORMS

An aluminium kettle appears to be in motion, as does a table protector called *Cool It*. The curvaceous lines spill across the surface. Parisian-born Stephane P. Rondel commenced his design business at the end of the 1980s. Having an engineering background, it's not surprising that his designs are not only aesthetically rewarding, but highly functional.

Working closely with the computer, each line of a product is mathematically perfected. Rondel's *Fire Box*, which consists of two perfectly symmetrical forms, was derived from the one mould. The box, which splits open to reveal a cast-iron rib cage, can be used as an oven, a smoker, a barbecue and even as a garden

incinerator. The tusk handle, which Rondel incorporates into his many interior projects, shows the same fluidity of his designs. 'The handle was designed to be bold without being severe and staunch without being overpowering,' he says. Unlike many handles that clearly show the bolt fixtures, Rondel's tusk appears to float on a glass door.

Rondel's *Table Cloth* defies description. Made entirely by computer, it's conception was the only human contribution. The *Table Cloth* was conceived and produced without being touched by human hands. The height and the diameter was entered and the computer did the rest. Even the creases, folds and the weight of the material were decided by the computer. Like honey, *Table Cloth* spills gently onto the floor. Even the simple coat hook is turned into a piece of fine sculpture. The elongated horns create a form of artwork for the back of a door and is extremely

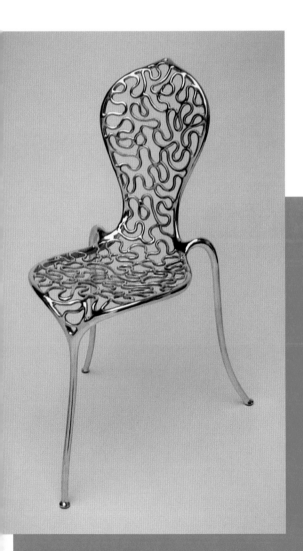

utilitarian. 'The *Antler Hook* will hold heavier items like bathrobes and damp towels,' he says. Like many of Rondel's designs, one form can find a number of applications. The *Antler Hook*, for example, can be used as a double-sided toilet roll holder or as a fixed door handle.

Each piece actually works rather than being conceived only for the pleasure of design. There is an exceptional quality to the work. As Rondel says, 'I'm anti consumer product. I'm for lifetime guarantee'.

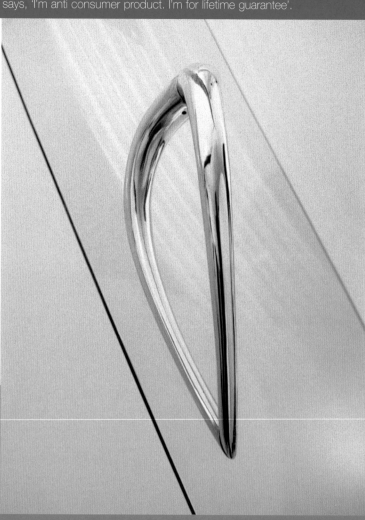

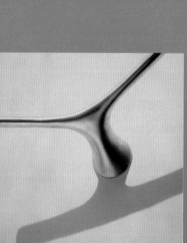

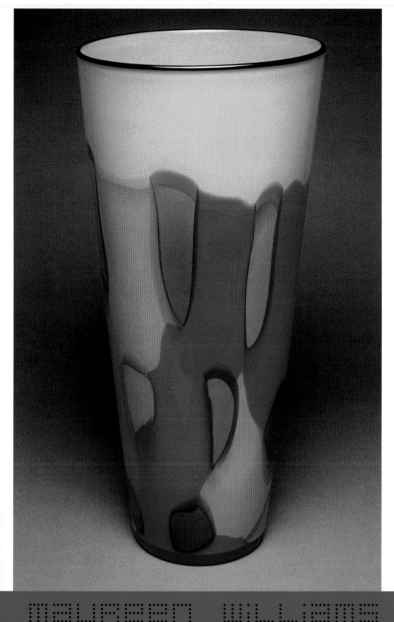

MAUREEN WILLIAMS – LUMINOUS FORMS

Glass vessels act as a canvas for artist Maureen Williams. Williams' glass vessels have a consistency with their fine elongated proportions. As Williams says, 'I use the vessel as a three-dimensional canvas, as a vehicle to express personal narratives. The images are in fact those of my dreams. The paintings are about the relationships between things, about social relationships. It's about how things touch and bump and move and go away again, and some never touch at all'.

Working with hot glass and paint in the same process, the brushstrokes become animated on the surface as the glass stretches and grows while being blown. 'The glass blanks or parisons are made, cooled and then painted with Paradise paint. These are then reheated, picked up on the blowing iron and covered with successive gathers of clear glass,' Williams says. While the mystical landscapes appear as spontaneous brushstrokes on each vessel, there are months spent thinking about each process. 'I spend months drawing, painting, reading and drawing on my influences,' she says.

Like the luminous and three-dimensional vases of Lalique, there is depth and richness to Williams' designs. Given the intricacy of each piece, it's not surprising that Williams works with a small team of glassblowers to assist her. As mentioned by Suzie Attiwill, a curator and lecturer in interior design at RMIT, 'The breath which animates the glass and extends the form is full and hearty. Wonderful lumps and a certain unwieldy exuberance invigorate the work'.

With titles such as *Journey 3*, *Journey Within a Journey 1* and *Simultaneous Voyage 3*, one is drawn into the experience of travelling and exploring the clouded landscapes. For Williams' *Coloured Series* the vessels

are inspired by abstract paintings. 'The colours are ordered to provide visual and technical balance, with each piece of colour individually applied to a clear glass parison using a torch and tweezers. They are slowly melted in, joined to form the colour abstract image and then free blown,' she says.

Like the forms which 'touch and bump' around the vessels, Williams touches the viewer with her unique visions, allowing them to take their own journeys in their own minds.

Robert Knottenbelt's glass sculptures appear at first to be from another galaxy. Like Martians that have just landed on our planet, the figurative forms stop you in your tracks. The watery structures, which include a number of rhythmic layers, convey a sense of urgency. For Knottenbelt, the urgency isn't visitors from another planet, but the important life forms on earth that face extinction.

The head of an albatross, made of plate glass that has been sandblasted and acid polished, finds a resting place after its travels. 'I've been following the plight of the sub-Arctic great wandering albatross populations from the impact of long-line fishing in the sub-Indian Ocean,' says Knottenbelt of his work titled *Antarctic Ghost Nest Dreaming*.

With the same careful observation, Knottenbelt could sense the frantic behaviour of human beings as they approached the end of the millennium. For the sculpture called *Milleniapede*, the figurative rows are out of step. A spanner has been thrown into the once rhythmic parade. 'This work is an attempt to describe that frantic late-20th century millennial feeling of running all over the place to no point in particular, rushing around like totally demented millipedes,' he says. Likewise, the work titled *The Prophet* also addresses the future. 'As a species, we always have speculative

hungers and concerns with what may happen in the immediate and the distant future,' he says.

For Knottenbelt, the inspiration for his work comes from a number of sources. With a strong interest since childhood in literature, science, politics and biology, it is not surprising that the issues presented in the sculptures come from a variety of sources. With the use of computer-generated imagery, the journeys taken by Knottenbelt have become more intricate, difficult and complicated than even he would have imagined.

However, the more difficult the journey for Knottenbelt, the more intriguing the forms become. As the sculptor says, 'It has allowed me the privilege to travel on my own, without mentors, without companions and to do things others have not done before. It's a real and rare pleasure'.

ROBERT KNOTTENBELT – MULTI-LAYERED

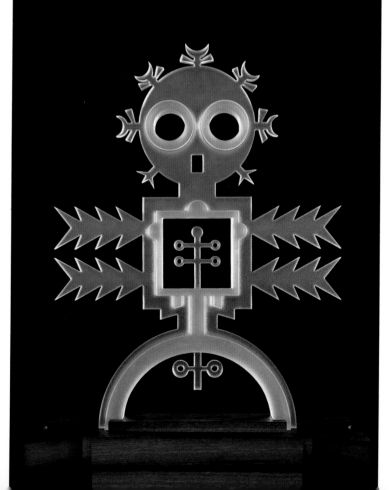

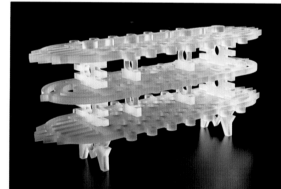

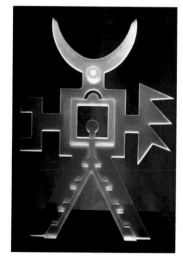

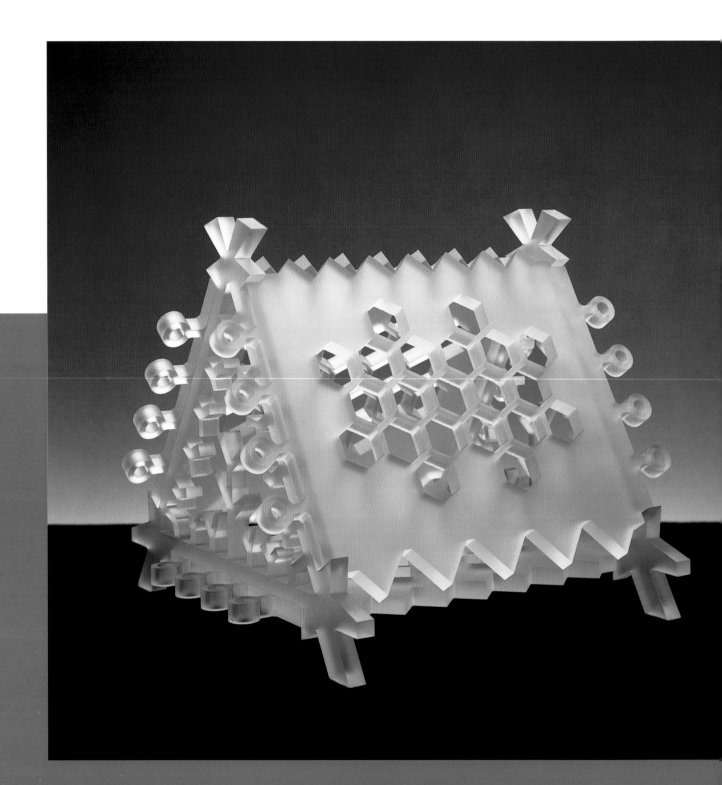

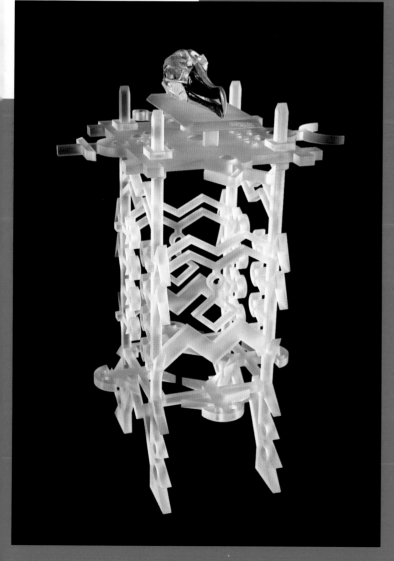

sculpture

Sculptor Geoffrey Bartlett may not be a household name, yet his work is regularly seen by thousands. In the moat outside the National Gallery of Victoria and as a beacon above one of Melbourne's apartment towers, Bartlett's work is part of our urban environment.

One of Bartlett's first large commissions came in the form of *The Messenger* (1983). The large painted steel sculpture, which measures 7x8x3 metres, was commissioned as a result of the Ian Potter Prize. 'There was a feeling at the time that the gallery had to be

identified and provide more of an indication of what was behind the bluestone walls,' Bartlett says. *The Messenger* not only provided a dialogue and a contrast to its bluestone backdrop, but raised the profile of contemporary sculpture in Australia.

Unlike many other art forms and areas of design that have a relatively short incubation period, Bartlett's work can take considerable time to emerge. 'With the size of many of the pieces, storage and space is obviously important. However, even when you get over that hurdle, the ideas and the form it takes can be a long process,' he says. The longevity of the process may help to explain the materials used, such as steel. One of the

GEOFFREY BARTLETT - ICONIC SCULPTURE

60

keys to unlocking some of the imagery in Bartlett's work is his use of contrasting elements. Organic materials such as timber are finely juxtaposed with manufactured materials such as galvanised iron inlaid with copper nails. 'There's an element of tension with the materials and their placement is crucial,' he says. One of Bartlett's more recent works, *The Obelisk* (1997) shows the architectural strength of the work. Capping a plain city apartment tower, Bartlett's sculpture acts as a jewel in the building's crown.

Whether the sculpture takes the form of a dancer or a self-portrait, Bartlett does not want the forms to be evident. 'I want my work to be interpreted in a variety of ways'. Those who might be in awe of Bartlett's work or even slightly ill-at-ease when confronted by the work in a gallery, find the

process of creation engaging. 'When people come into my studio and see the process of how the sculpture is made, there's more of a connection. They're generally less intimidated,' he says. While Bartlett's sculpture is now part of Australia's urban fabric, the artist behind the monumental work largely remains unidentified from those passing by.

63

64

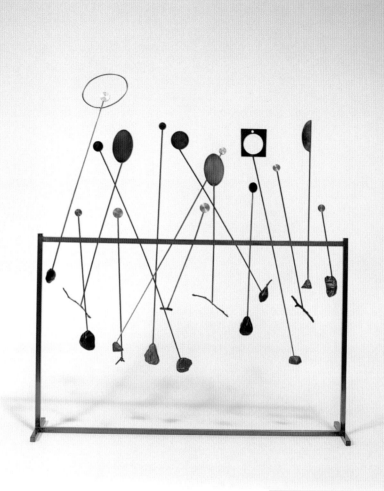

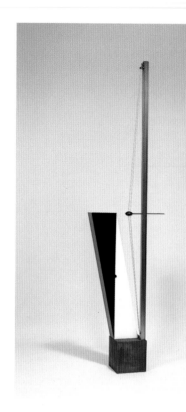

PETER D COLE - FINE LINES

The sculptures of Peter D Cole have always attracted favourable reviews, even when they were extremely minimal in the late 1960s. 'My early work was very minimal. I was working with many throwaway materials such as rope, glass and latex. There was very little form to the work,' Cole says.

The depth that Cole was looking for in his sculpture started to emerge with many social issues, both at home and abroad. The Iranian crisis at the start of the 1980s is finely captured in his work, *Mosque-attack*, where the turret of a Mosque is substituted for a rocket. Likewise, the Pentagon is featured in another work, with six rocket-like minarets emerging from the iconic building. 'I wanted to create a duality of images but I was also interested in Islamic architecture,' Cole says.

The materials in Cole's sculptures include brass, bronze, steel and aluminium. 'Metal is not only a hardy material, but is a medium that when painted, doesn't rust. It allows me to be more expressive, and unlike wood, allows me to create the same fine lines that I can create on paper'. While the work from sculptors such as Henry Moore can take years to

complete due to the nature of their material (stone), Cole's sculpture can be conceived in a matter of days. 'I like to have a fairly instant result. The basis of one of my pieces can be put down in a few days and then slowly refined. I want my sculptures to be almost transparent, like handwriting that is defined by the placement of its letters and the spaces in between,' Cole says. Cole often makes a number of components in his work well in advance of their placement. 'I might make a number of individual components and play around with them for a few weeks'.

Based in Kyneton, an hour's drive out of Melbourne, it's not difficult to see where many of the influences on Cole's work come from. Cole's sculpture *Rocks and Stars*, in painted and patinated brass, bronze and stainless steel, reflects the natural terrain around

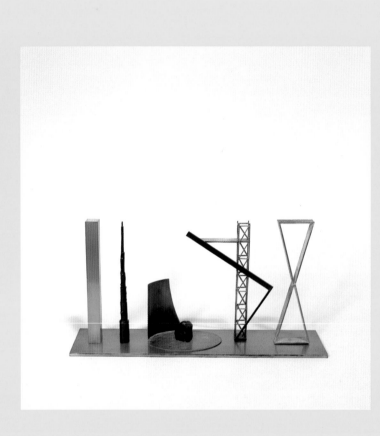

Kyneton. 'I create a lot of figurative pieces, but many capture the elements in the landscape, the rocks, the sun and the moon'. However, Cole moves beyond the physical elements in a landscape, capturing the sounds and movements that are rarely witnessed. Cole's work, *Trees and bird's nest*, graphically captures the movement of a bird, with its journey from the hollow of a tree to a branch. The reduction, whether a landscape or a bird's travel, not only captures the subject, but creates powerful imagery in the process.

One of Australia's most prolific and celebrated sculptors, Inge King, made her mark on the urban fabric during the post-war period. 'It is the Australian landscape that grips my imagination and is the main source of my inspiration. I try to measure my work against the vast spaces of this country,' King says. While the scale of King's sculpture is daunting for those who pass by her work, it isn't the size that captures the sculptor's imagination. 'The simplicity and clarity of the form expressing its inner strength and tension, that is the motivating force. I see my sculptures as part of the environment. I want people to be challenged by the forms and arouse their curiosity to explore them,' she says.

King's *Forward Surge*, commissioned for the Victorian Arts Centre and installed in 1981, highlighted both the importance and significance of sculpture and the artist's work to Australia. The wave-like shapes contrast with the verticality of the high-rise buildings that frame the work. While each new work is meticulously planned, there is always a sense of trepidation before each sculpture arrives in its new surroundings. 'Seeing the sculpture finally in place on a beautiful sunny Autumn day, the arches soaring into the sky, and linking the two buildings, spire and concert hall, was a wonderful experience,' King says.

A more recent work, titled *Sentinel*, made of 10-millimetre polychrome steel plates, casts a watchful eye over a Melbourne freeway. The organic black vertical forms, which compose the body of the sculpture, provide a contrast to the road signs and light poles of the surrounding area.

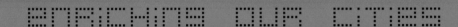

INGE KING – ENRICHING OUR CITIES

'The multi-coloured crown is the focal point of the work. Its curved shapes symbolise the two creeks of the municipality (City of Manningham), the Mullum Mullum and the Koonung creeks,' she says. The vibrant colours allow not only the motorists to appreciate the sculpture, but also residents living in the distance and overlooking the freeway.

King trained in Germany and Great Britain before settling in Australia and it's not surprising to find her work spanning the continent. Whether King's extraordinary sculpture finds its way into a city location or on the suburban fringe, the built environment is greatly enriched. As King says, 'My hope is to involve the passer-by in the sculpture, stimulate their imagination by adding their own interpretation'.

AUGUSTINE DALL'AVA
– A SENSE OF THE SURREAL

For sculptor Augustine Dall'Ava, intuition plays an important role in his work. While there is a spontaneity in the designs, each piece requires considerable time to evolve. Instead of focusing on one piece at a time, Dall'Ava moves around his studio and attends to each sculpture as it slowly moves towards completion. 'Having a number of works in different stages of progress gives me more time for contemplation, change and finally a greater degree of resolution,' he says.

The strong primary colours which are used in Dall'Ava's sculptures not only reflect the artist's Mediterranean background, but help to create an entirely different mood in each component. Born in France, to Italian parents, Dall'Ava spent years working various jobs in Australia before turning to studying sculpture at RMIT. Later travels to Japan were a significant influence on his work. The beauty of the traditional Japanese gardens, with their sensitive use of materials, their sense of calm understatement, and their evident spiritual quality reinforced his existing interest in the use of natural materials and processes.

The elements which appear frequently in Dall'Ava's work, such as clouds, stones, moon, seed pods, branches and fruit, are used in an ambiguous manner to create their own moods. 'Rocks normally belong at the beach. You can find thousands there. However, you can remove them from their context and elevate them to another level. On a stand, it's no longer just another pebble on the beach,' he says.

As sculptor Celia Winter-Irving says, 'Dall'Ava has a gleeful sense of invention. He turns the humble pebble into a feisty little warmonger, with the addition of spiky combs. Plastic snails lay their trails in small boxes and lock their horns in combat. He plays a game of brinkmanship with configuration, his objects hover on the edge of representation, his trees dance on the margins of the literal'.

While Dall'Ava continually sketches, he prefers to work with his sculptures in a more intuitive manner. 'There's not just one idea that comes from nowhere. I'm continually inspired by numerous experiences, from nature and from the work of other artists. There's not a particular theory,' he says.

74

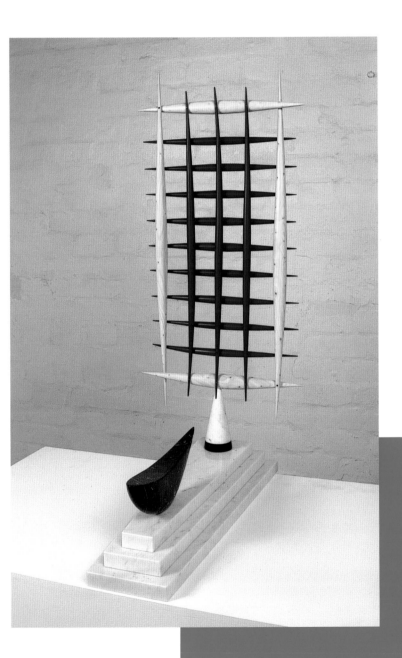

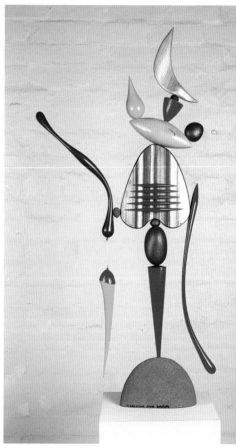

The work of sculptor Robert Bridgewater invites the viewer to touch and caress each piece. The elaborate patterns carved into the timbers emphasise the labour spent manipulating the environment. The timber forms, which are either painted or bleached, have a force of their own. 'I use patterns that I find recurring in art and design objects, from various cultures and periods of history, to explore the range of relationships between form and pattern. I particularly like to use the patterns from nature, the leaves, the scales, wool and water,' Bridgewater says.

Bridgewater, who sees his work as fitting somewhere in the tradition of landscape art, is mindful of the process of labour that goes into each piece of work. 'I remember studying an antique Chinese urn in art history as a student. It wasn't just the craftsmanship that went into making that urn 2000 years ago, but the way it communicated another period and the manual labour that went into it,' he says. Two thousand years down the track, Bridgewater's own sculptures immediately evoke the same diligence and labour of his own hands. One can almost witness Bridgewater's hands at work as he finely chisels away the timber.

ROBERT BRIDGEWATER
- CARVING OUT A NAME

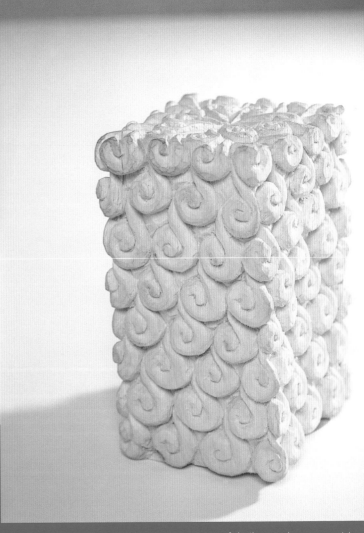

The *Vertical Group* which features the *Beard, Quilted Trunk, Smokescreen, Volcano and Aileron*, vary in height up to 2.5 metres. Displayed mounted to the wall or on the ground, each work is covered in elaborate patterns. 'There's a stillness in the grouping. It's that kind of stillness of grown trees that have been isolated over time,' he says. For Bridgewater, who was born near the small rural town of Nhill in Western Victoria, the use of timber is a continual reminder of his background. 'I lived on a farm right on the edge of the Little Desert National Park. What was appropriate land use and what wasn't appropriate was always an issue. A lot of my work is about the relationship between cultural, man-made things and natural things'.

The carved patterns not only create a sense of rhythm and movement to the work, but also accentuate the volumes, the tension and the flexibility of the material. As Bridgewater says, 'I try to design forms to be elusive, but with a suggestion that they do refer to a range of objects from the natural and manufactured worlds'. Like the ancient Chinese urn that allows the past to unfold, Bridgewater's exquisite sculptures will be clearly heard by future generations.

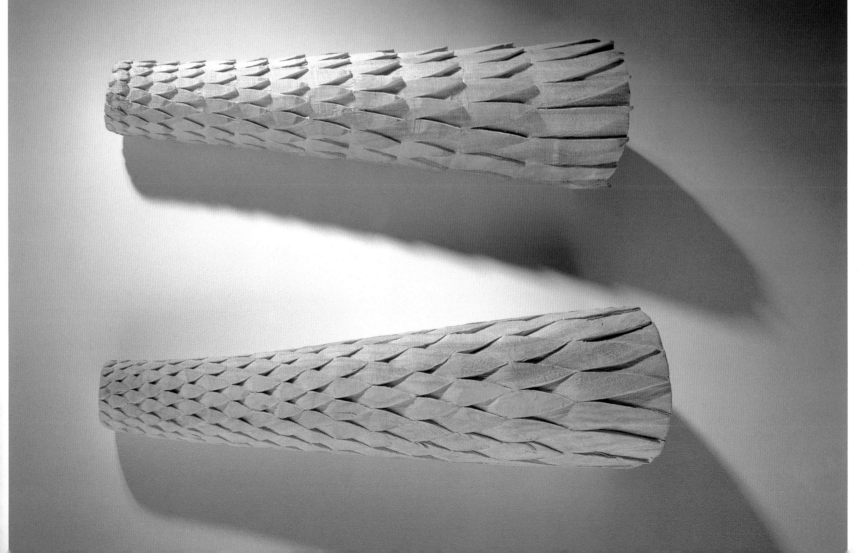

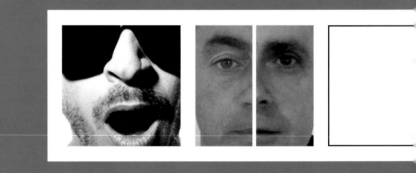

furniture

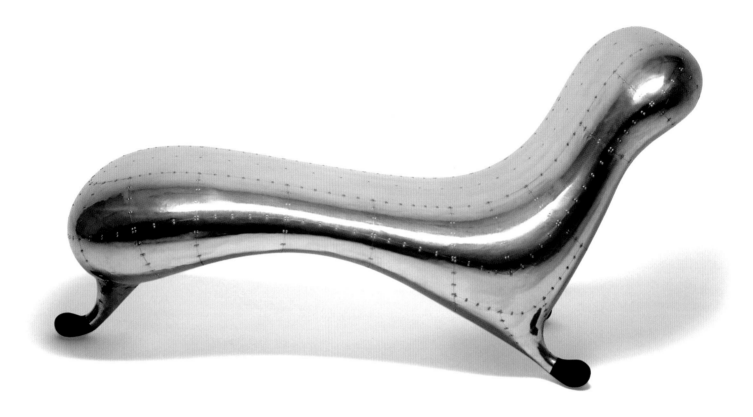

MARC NEWSON - A HOUSEHOLD NAME

When Madonna performed her hit single *Rain*, it wasn't only the lyrics that vibrated through television sets around the world. As powerful an image was the *Lockhead Lounge LC2* designed by Marc Newson that shimmered in the background. The peanut-shaped lounge made of fibreglass and aluminium was designed with only three legs. Resembling an industrial object rather than a comfortable lounge to relax in, the *Lockhead*, designed in 1988, was one of a number of pieces to jettison Newson into the international design arena.

Born in Sydney, Australia, Newson spent his childhood travelling in Europe and Asia before studying jewellery and sculpture at the Sydney College of the Arts. Newson started experimenting with furniture design as a student. Unlike many designers who may wait years before their work is noticed, it wasn't long after graduation that Teruo Kurosaki, a Japanese entrepreneur, showed interest in manufacturing Newson's designs for his company Idee. Newson's *Orgone Lounge*, *Black Hole Table* and *Felt Chair* were taken off the drawing board. By the early 1990s, with a studio in Paris, Newson was receiving major commissions from prestigious European manufacturers such as Flos for lighting and Cappellini and Moroso for furniture.

For Newson, his most preferred method of designing is with a pen and a small notepad. 'It's all conceived in my head to start with, from the shape to the type of material I want to use. I can't imagine sitting down at a desk and trying to chase an idea,' he says. Whether the design is for a chair, a watch, a restaurant or an apartment block, there is an unmistakable signature that clearly reads as Newson.

If one was to doubt the value of Newson's designs, you need only read the recently reported news that one of his *Lockhead* lounges sold at a Christie's Auction in New York for US$105,000. Collected by museums and galleries around the world, Newson must be considered one of the most accomplished and influential designers of his generation.

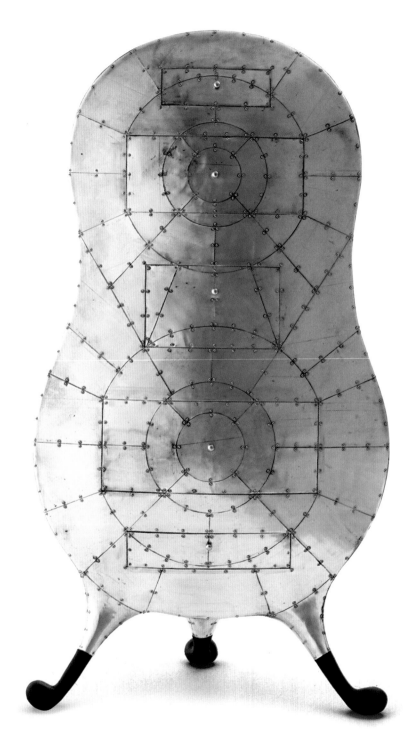

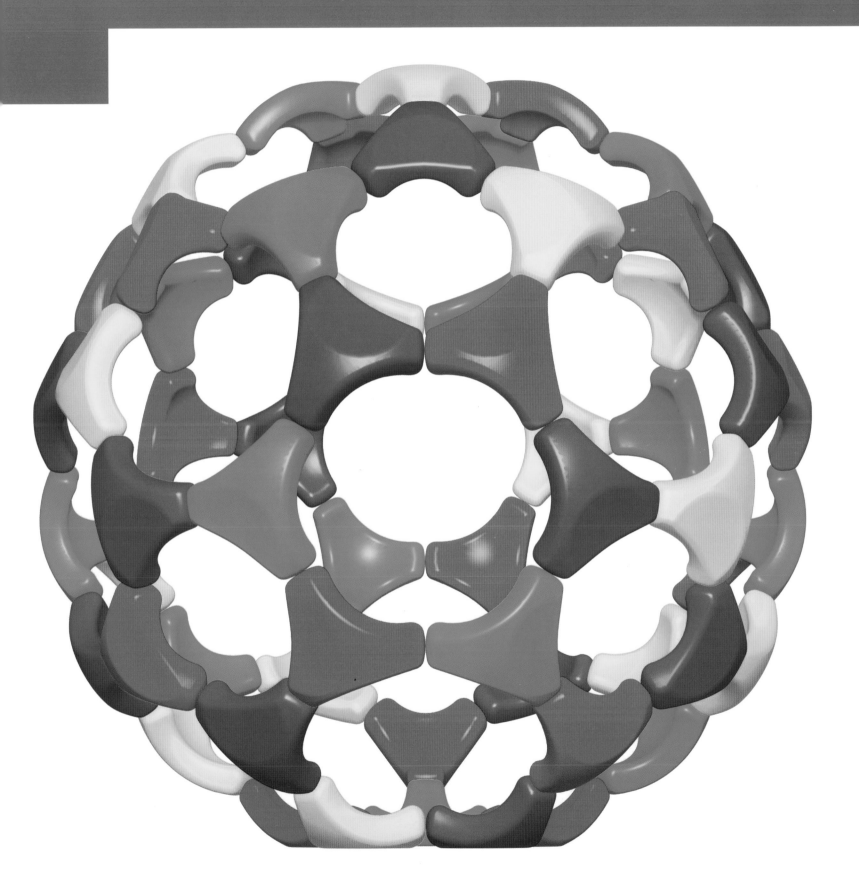

When architects went down the minimalist road in the 1990s, the sparse interiors they produced required only a few pieces of furniture. It's therefore not surprising that only the talented furniture designers made an appearance on the concrete floors of that period. For Christopher Connell and Raoul C. Hogg, who formed MAP at the start of the 1990s, the minimal lines and white walls that were favoured by architects helped to showcase their furniture.

When the *Pepe* chair appeared in 1993, architects and designers were keen to have their latest project photographed with the *Pepe*. The organic-shaped chair,

made of a tubular-steel frame engulfed by polyurethane foam in a mould, has a moveable back rest. The wool-covered chairs, which come in a range of sumptuous colours, have not only become icon pieces of furniture, but have helped put the design practice on the MAP. While it has been the *Pepe* that has attracted media attention, it is the full range of functional and simple furniture that finds its way into some of Australia's leading contemporary interiors. The simple *Oak* chair is as timeless as the *Slab*, with most designs being incorporated into both commercial and domestic projects.

'Essentially, we get the idea onto paper and try and capture the spontaneity of the initial concept. Simplicity is the utmost importance to our design ethic. We try and do more with less,' Connell says.

MAP – THAT EDGE

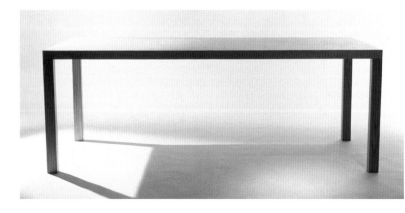

While a number of designers might scour the market and look for areas of deficiency, MAP are not driven by the market, but are mindful of directions. 'We would never say let's design a chair because the market dictates this design. Raoul and I are continually discussing ideas and exploring new materials and techniques,' he says.

MAP are spending more of their energy designing rather than manufacturing and filling their showroom to the rafters. A large screen on the showroom wall featuring the entire range reduces the need to show every piece designed over the years. While the thought of a showroom without furniture has a certain appeal, it's perhaps taking the idea of minimalism too far. As Hogg says, 'An important part of buying furniture is the tactile experience. People need to see the quality and appreciate the comfort factor'.

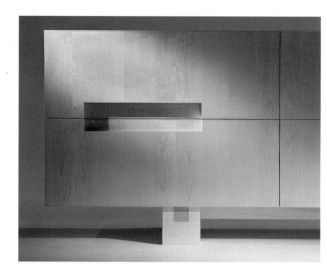

Metallurgy may seem a long way from furniture design, however, for designer Paul Morris of Join, the years spent in metallurgy gave him a new perspective to designing and manufacturing furniture. 'The course (at La Trobe University in Bendigo) gave me an appreciation of how materials behave and react together. It really puts you into a research mode and helps you think laterally,' Morris says.

Join, which started in 1996, began with the idea of creating furniture that had quality as its underlying premise. When you look at the Join range of furniture, a timeless quality pervades, with all the fine details carefully resolved. 'I don't particularly like the word craftsmanship as it conjures up furniture that is usually antique or from a period. What I'm particularly interested in is developing systems, which includes people, materials, communication and administration; developing a system to ensure the product's success,' he says.

One of the first pieces that was designed by Join was the *rombi* (square). Covered in vibrant brushed cottons from chartreuse to fuschia, the *rombi* adds colour to any room. Despite its size, the *rombi* is more comfortable than many lounge chairs on the market. The *rombi* bench, which developed out of the square, is ideal for sprawling out with the newspaper. One of Join's hallmarks is the absence of handles. 'When you start using handles that might appear on other products in the market, it takes the

JOIN - FINELY CRAFTED

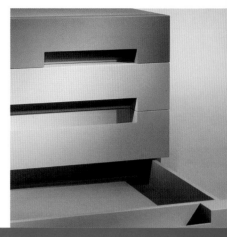

identity or uniqueness away from that piece. Sometimes, it often looks like an afterthought,' Morris says. As a substitute for handles, Morris devised his own built-in handles that take their cue from the shape and function of the piece of furniture. Another important feature to Join's approach to design is the scale of each piece. 'Furniture is usually seen from the angle of sitting down. I prefer people not to be overwhelmed by furniture, whether visually or practically. It also creates a feeling of space'.

Other Join designs include the *fat file*, made of Medium-Density Fibreboard in subtle beige and brown tones and the *toshi* (low). The thought behind each design is as refreshing as the design itself. As Morris says, 'If people are living in an apartment or small terrace, the traditional dining table may not be appropriate. The toshi becomes the one table in the space'.

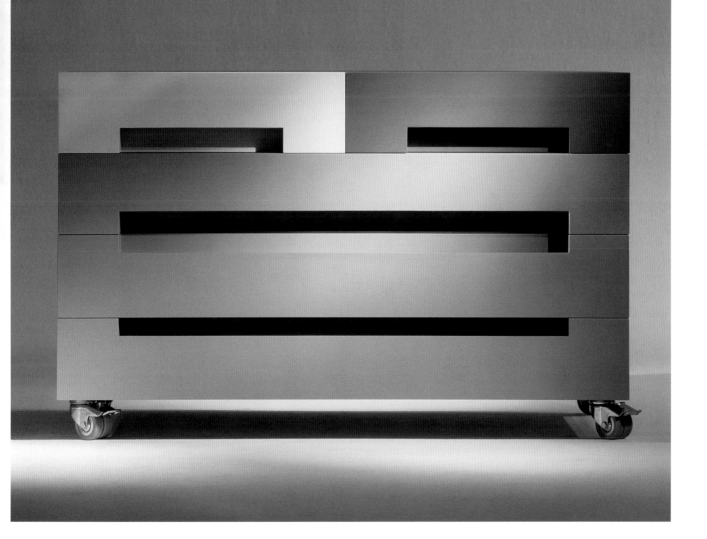

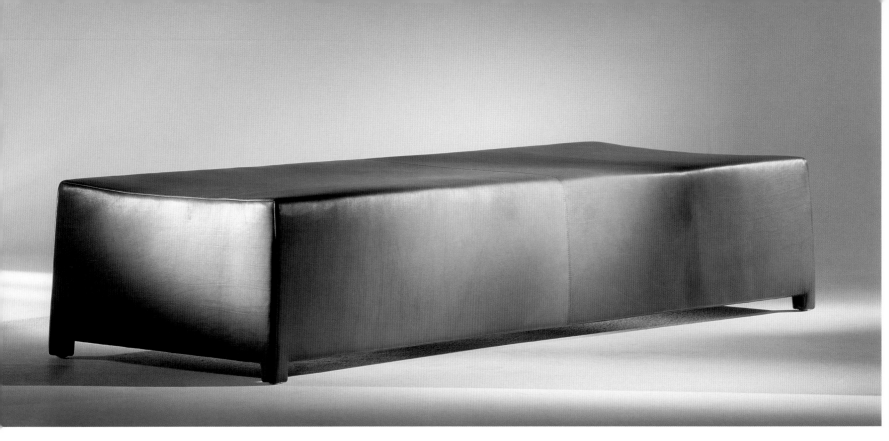

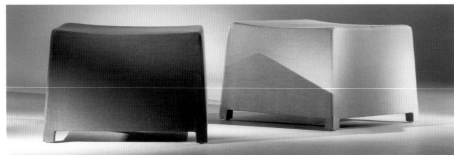

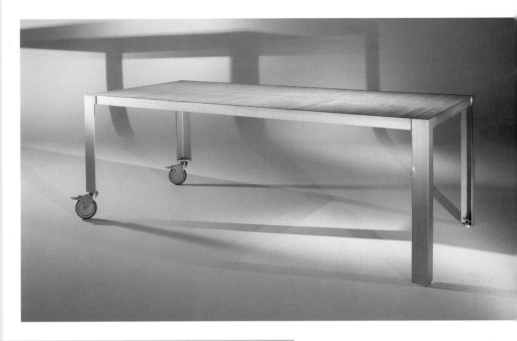

CAROLINE CASEY – NEW HORIZONS

When Caroline Casey walked into Anibou, one of Sydney's leading furniture retailers more than five years ago, the word quickly spread. Armed only with a portfolio of drawings and models of furniture, Casey's talent was easily recognised. 'It wasn't just the quality of the drawings and the models, but the breadth of her ideas,' Anibou's Manager Ute Rose says.

Five years later, with numerous exhibitions to Casey's credit and her furniture collected by museums and galleries around Australia and internationally, Rose's instinct has proven accurate. After years of producing in Australia, Casey is about to manufacture and supply retailers in Germany. Casey's *Zella* day bed and

The Wishbone clothes ladder, which featured in the German design magazine *Architektur & Wohnen* (Architecture & Lifestyle), will now be appreciated by a much larger audience.

While Casey's range of furniture is extensive (more than 25 pieces), it is the more unusual pieces that cause the greatest reaction. 'There's more of a demand for the more unusual pieces that are unique,' Casey says. Whatever form Casey's furniture takes, whether it's her *Tina* tables, her *Elliptical* folding screen or her *Ned* bins, revealing the essence of an object and its underlying structure continues to play an important role in her designs. 'With the Zella day bed for example, the rawness of the material is expressed underneath,' she says. For Ute Rose, it is that simplicity and refinement that makes Casey's work so unique. 'Caroline really cuts back her designs to the basics. She cuts back to the essentials of a piece and

refrains from including anything superfluous to that design'. Whether it is the *Elliptical* screen or a coffee table, there is a rhythm and a sense of movement to the designs which are finely resolved.

While the venture into Germany will add a new dimension to Casey's work, the desire to slow down the design process is rarely considered. 'I'm interested in working with new materials and with new technology. It improves your design capabilities and presents new challenges. Weaving with industrial steel is one of the possibilities I am exploring. I also want to continue to explore traditional techniques in contemporary forms,' Casey says.

For designers Marc Schamburg and Michael Alvisse, designing furniture goes well beyond the aesthetics. The issues regarding the manufacturing process are as crucial as the design itself.

The firm's commitment to a sustainable environment was recently highlighted in the *4 + 1* exhibition, at Sydney's Powerhouse Museum. 'We exhibited the *stretch* stool which was made of polyester resin. In a sense we exhibited a piece that we considered failed in terms of its manufacturing process. It required the handling of toxic chemicals,' says designer Michael Alvisse. Rather than continue to produce the stretch in polyester resin, the duo turned to recycled plastics. 'It's environmentally neutral without the toxic chemical,' he says.

The simple *Bummegg* stool, which was recently added to the designers' range, was inspired by the hardboiled chicken egg. Designed with a polypropylene shell, the stool is counterbalanced by a weighted rubber base. As Alvisse says, 'The user is invited to interact with the piece to achieve a dynamic state of ergonomically desirable balance'. While new ideas are always evolving at Schamburg + Alvisse, the emphasis is continually on research and development. 'We're particularly interested in

new materials, particularly the new plastics which are sustainable and have a life beyond their product. The product could be melted down or used to form a new product down the line,' Alvisse says.

'The other area of concern to this firm is looking at the human systems that generate the product in the first place. We're interested in how the key people in the design organisation structure the workload, making sure that the systems are in place to create a thriving workplace,' Alvisse says. While exhibitions are still firmly on the agenda, so is the desire to continually explore the design and manufacturing process. Like the *Stretch* range of furniture that helped to establish the Schamburg + Alvisse name, the ideas and ingenuity of this firm appear endless.

SCHAMBURG + ALVISSE
– WELL BEYOND AESTHETICS

111

TIM MILLER - OBJECTS OF DESIRE

Two simple materials, corrugated iron and timber, are cleverly brought together in the work of New Zealand designer Tim Miller. With the penetration of the corrugated iron into the timber-surfaced bench, a fascinating dialogue is created. The ripples of the iron create a new perspective for the simple timber bench. These common materials are transformed into objects of desire.

For Miller, who worked with a number of leading furniture design organisations in the UK before emigrating to New Zealand, defining a sense of place has always been important. The *Good Feed* storage system, also made of timber and roofing materials, expresses New Zealand's agricultural heritage. 'I wanted to express some of the qualities of this country's materials and to explore the contrast between the open

and closed cabinet,' Miller says. 'Closed, the corrugated iron wall acts as a veil of expectation. The tranquil rippled plane is broken by evocative feeding teats attracting the touch, which surprisingly transforms them into door handles. Farm buildings were the inspiration for both the material's colour and texture,' he says.

Miller has for the past 10 years had a strong interest in CAD, particularly with 3D modelling. As a lecturer in Industrial Design at the Victoria University of Wellington, Miller teaches his students the value of computers to aid creative design activities. 'I'm particularly interested

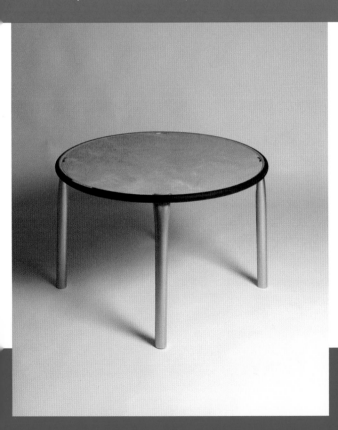

in computer aided manufacturing, which is going to give architects and industrial designers more opportunities and freedom in the future'.

The *Rino Bench* has been developed for Te Papa (The Museum of New Zealand), where 21 benches have been installed in the public spaces (the word *Rino* is Maori for iron). While iron is generally used as a roofing material, the specific iron used by Miller is

0.55 millimetres thick, giving the *Rino* its required strength. 'An additional non-load bearing sheet is folded into the leg to gain further longitudinal rigidity,' Miller says.

While from the outset Miller's designs appear simple; the mechanics to each piece are as fascinating as the designs themselves. As Miller says, referring to *A Good Feed*, 'Some corrugated troughs on the cabinet doors contain external hinge fittings that use modern roofing screws. These are contrasted internally by traditional cabinetmaker's butt hinges'. Exploring Miller's work is more than a substitute for a good feed.

Tim Miller and David Trubridge are part of a group of New Zealand Designers called Loop Group, which sells ideas and products from New Zealand.

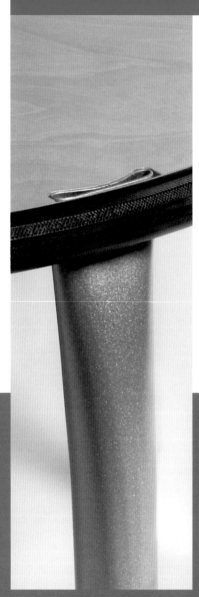

115

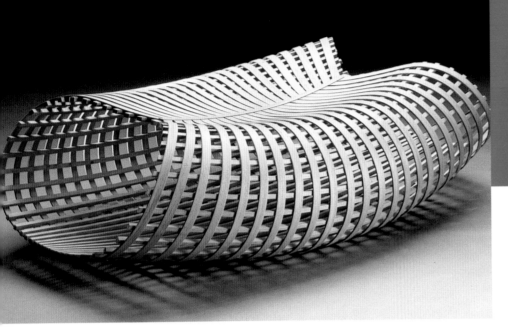

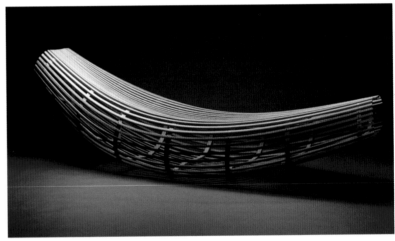

DAVID TRUBRIDGE
... A SENSE OF EXPLORATION

For New Zealand-based furniture designer David Trubridge there is a continual desire to explore structures. Instead of starting with the notion of producing a chair or a table and following a design brief, the impetus is more emotive. 'I don't see the point of making just another dining room chair. There might be a new detail in my chair, but that won't sustain my interest in furniture,' Trubridge says.

Trubridge, who originally trained as a naval architect at university, began designing furniture which had a strong contemporary edge. Like an artist who turns to life drawing to explore the figurative form, Trubridge sees his designs as similar to the artistic process of creation. 'My tables often take the appearance of a figure supporting a bowl, instead of four legs and a uniform surface. However, there's still an element of function to the pieces that makes the piece furniture rather than a piece of art or sculpture,' he says. There is a remnant of functionality that deems it to be furniture. 'My furniture does raise the question of whether it is art or sculpture. I'm interested in it being used, but it's designed from an emotive response rather than following the more traditional design process,' he says.

The *Body Raft* series, which has formed part of a number of international exhibitions, shows the fluidity of Trubridge's work, together with the exploration of the structures that inspire him. 'The first *Body Rafts* were

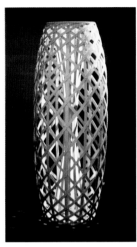

quite complex. They were probably over designed,' Trubridge says. The rafts made of elm or ash are steam bent. With the last *Raft* that was made, the ends were simply truncated. As Trubridge says, 'The eye can easily continue the lines. In your mind you can extend the form. I aim to create sufficiently abstract forms to allow the viewer plenty of opportunity to discover their own connections'.

David Trubridge's furniture might not sit perfectly around the dining room table. Likewise, his *Body Rafts* continue to appear as volatile as the waves. However, for Trubridge, the exploration is as important as the designs themselves.

New Zealand furniture designer Humphrey Ikin has always been intent on creating strong individual designs that reflect his own culture. Forms such as the indigenous canoe and ceremonial bowl can be read into his work. However, a show of Ikin's work titled *Facing North* spoke of the designer's intent. 'Each seeks out a striking profile under harsh lighting. Each work resolves its play of tensions around a clear axis ... Colour emphasises the serial nature of the pieces. It also functions to remove the seduction of the wood's grain from our sensory range,' says Giles Reid, who reviewed Iken's work for the exhibition.

Like the Dutch architect Gerrit Rietveld's *Red-and-blue Chair* that was designed in 1918, Ikin's designs also show a playful and sculptural form. The fine and elongated proportions of Ikin's *Tall Red Shelves* and the *Tall Dark Cabinet*, also recall the iconic work of Charles Rennie Mackintosh at the turn of the last century. 'I treat each piece as a prototype for production, whether it is created as a single piece or as a multiple. I also enjoy working across the continuum, from production design to sculpture,' Ikin says.

Instead of drawing one's attention to the timber used, whether rosewood or walnut, Ikin celebrates the wood grains within each piece, with the original lines and those added over time adding value to the piece. While the wood surface is painted, often in red and black, the colour skims the

HUMPHREY IKIN – CASTING SHADOWS

120

surface. 'I am particularly interested in the surface qualities of materials. I've explored this area of my work religiously, especially with wood. It's important to retain the visual clues to the material rather than over-relying on its seductive qualities,' he says.

Whether it's the *Red Table* or a non-coloured design such as the *Bench*, which is made of aluminium and oak, the designs have a strong sense of place in the Pacific region. Ikin's designs evoke a time when benches were carved from single tree trunks for the local tribes. However, they are clearly directed towards the future, with each of the pieces casting their own strong and well defined shadows.

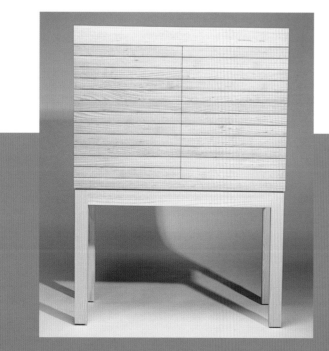

123

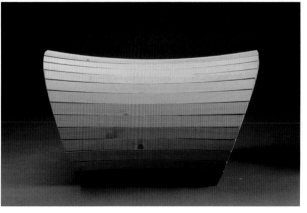

lighting

DENIS SMITKA - SIMPLE DETAIL

For Melbourne-based designer Denis Smitka, lighting became his medium of choice soon after graduating from RMIT. 'In the early 1990s, I was designing furniture and lighting while I was travelling around Europe. The ideas, which were about a dozen in total, formed a small portfolio on my return,' he says. The first range of lighting from Smitka was the *clio* range. This range, which featured a standard, a table and a pendant lamp, was the first commercial range he produced. Designed in reconstituted veneers, and more recently with new age veneers such as banksia, the lights are refined and understated.

With the demand for new products and for Smitka's own development, two new ranges have since been released, the *Mono* and the range of *Poli* lights. The *Mono* features handmade glass that is manufactured in Europe to Smitka's brief, while the *Poli* range is injection moulded. 'The *Poli* was designed in the form of separate thermoplastic modules that are then folded to form various sized shades. The height is fixed due to the tooling mechanisms, but the diameter and shape is flexible,' he says. The folded membrane of the *Poli* acts as a light filter, creating soft lighting without diminishing its strength. 'Light is the driving force when I'm designing a new range. The effect of the light is as important as its final form. With the *Mono* range the light disperses from the central point,' says Smitka.

Smitka emphasises the importance of three-dimensional exploration. 'You can have an idea, but you really need to see if it can be achieved in reality'. While his designs are sophisticated, the materials used are not precious. 'Often I add value to cheaper materials. With the *Poli* lighting range for example, the expense comes through the construction when folding each module. The table lamp requires 24 separate modules with the larger pendants taking up to 50 modules. I always try to reduce an idea down, but I don't want to lose its integrity'.

Instead of making a light a centrepiece to a room, Smitka prefers his designs to complement the interior. 'I don't want my lights to become striking art pieces that you notice as soon as you walk into a room. I prefer more subtle design'. While Smitka's lighting appears simple from the outset, a closer inspection reveals the fine details, from the careful folds to the fine aluminium brackets.

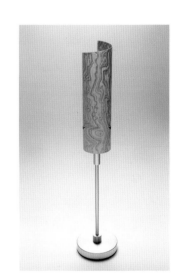

129

Designers Simon Christopher and Celina Clarke of ISM Objects have been experimenting with new lighting forms for many years. With smaller homes and apartments in mind, ISM Objects were interested in designing objects and lighting which could be bundled into a waiting taxi should the move be sudden. With a client base that also includes restaurants and hotels, ISM Objects' lighting is well embedded into the urban fabric.

The *Robo* range of lights, made of moulded polymer, reflect the shape of the contemporary interior, with a softer rounder edge. The *Robo* was designed as a pendant light, a flush wall light and a table lamp, in a range of colours from ice blue, pine lime and powder pink to opal. 'We couldn't create that rounded edge by using glass. Using the moulding process gives it that point of difference,' Clarke says. The other benefit with the process is its flexibility, with designers being able to customise multiple lights for larger projects such as a hotel. 'There's now a more handcrafted look to lighting that has its own character. Whatever form the light takes, it's important to get the quality of the light right,' she says. The *FAB* table lamp with its aluminium stem and white polymer shade is a classic example of ISM Objects' work, clean and simple lines created from a confident mixture of materials.

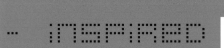

ISM OBJECTS
– INSPIRED BY THE MATERIALS AND TECHNOLOGY

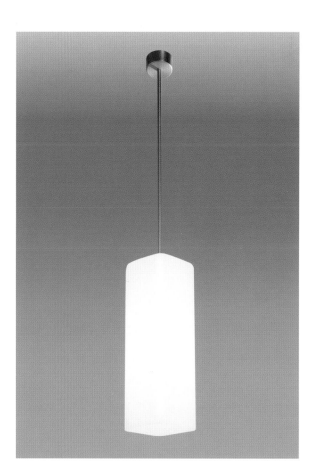

ISM believes that less is more and that often simplicity can deliver the best result. For this talented duo, inspiration is derived from an integrity in materials and technology. Mindful of the need to export their lighting, the designs can be dismantled in a cardboard flat pack. 'Our products are designed with export in mind. Everything intended for manufacture (as an ISM product) has to be price conscious, whether it is destined for the retail market or developed for commercial fit out. That's where design becomes an integral part of the process, producing a quality, cost-effective solution that utilises intelligence with both materials and technology,' Christopher says.

Collaborating with some of Australia's leading architects and designers is an important function at ISM Objects. With numerous awards for their designs, both in Australia and overseas, ISM's lights are refreshingly simple. The purity of their lines is rivalled only by the quality of the light.

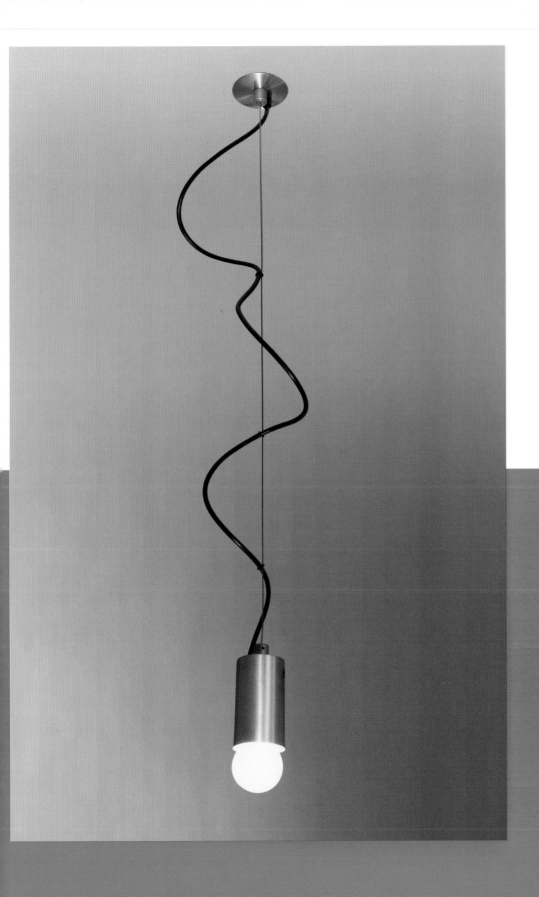

MARC PASCAL - M2 PRODUCTS

Initially graduating from the Victorian College of the Arts, designer Marc Pascal appears to have covered the whole design spectrum. 'While I'd always loved colour and drawing, the industrial design course at RMIT became the perfect vehicle to channel my energy'.

While some designers turn to the computer to initiate the design process, Pascal prefers to sketch out his ideas on large pieces of paper. The sketches are then translated to plaster or to foam which then take on a three-dimensional form. 'I draw and doodle and then I mock up one or two of the ideas'. Pascal's woven range of plastic lights are individually hand woven in an endless combination of subtle shades. 'The woven idea started out as a bag for my girlfriend, before moving into a form of lighting. I never thought that I would be weaving plastic,' Pascal says. With the dye cut plastic strips colour dyed in house, the client's order can be extremely specific. 'One of the *Worvo* lights was recently designed with cool colours

on one side and warm on the other. It enabled the light to be turned around to reflect a certain mood in the room,' he says.

The *Worvo* light is named from the words 'weave' and 'torso' (the light's resemblance to a shapely woman's form). The *Worvo*, in its three forms, the table, the standard and the pendant, has helped to illuminate showroom windows around Australia. As with many of Pascal's designs, one idea is later expressed with an entirely new spin. The multi-coloured plastic strips of the *Worvo* were also designed in the form of oversized woven panels that are back lit. Art and lighting are brought together in the process.

Whether the design takes the form of a light or appears in the shape of a clock, a fruit bowl or a six-pronged ceramic vase, Pascal's work shows a strong character. The *Bulbous Flex* pendant shade, which is made from dye cut and laser cut plastics, shows his preference for organic shaped forms and for materials that aren't fragile. As Pascal says, 'Being a Taurean, I am sensual, emotive and tactile. I like to marry form with function and material. I aim to find a balance between practicality and aesthetics. Finding the most appropriate materials and ways of utilising these leads to the solutions'.

140

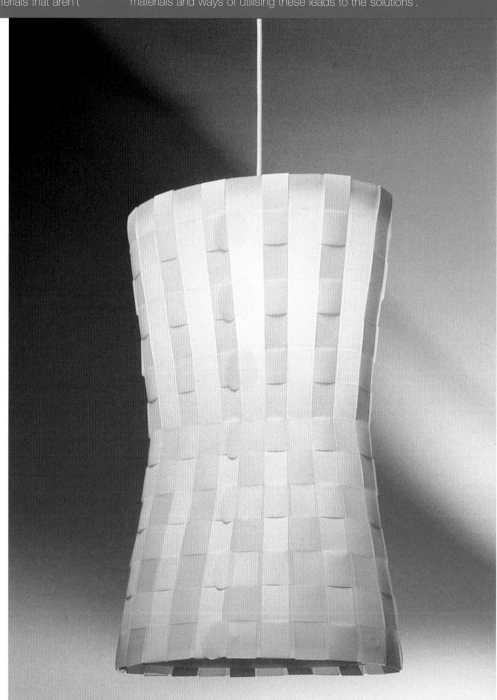

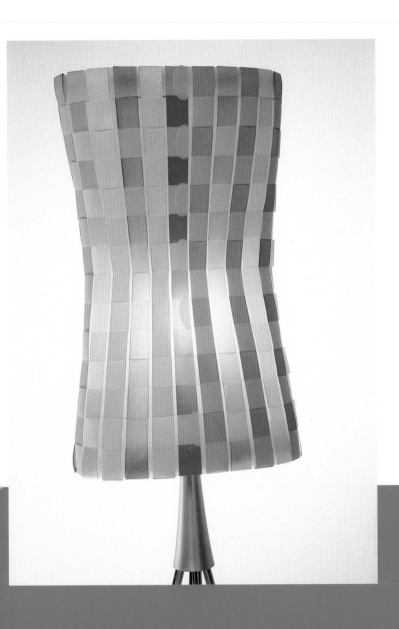

Interior designer Marc Schamburg and architect Michael Alvisse have made a name for themselves in the area of furniture design. However, given their talent in numerous design areas, it is not surprising that lighting has featured in their more recent ranges.

The floor lamp, named the *Regalo di Canto*, was recently exhibited at the Salone del Mobili in Milan. The light not only attracted a continual stream of onlookers, but helped focus the international press towards Australian and New Zealand design.

Measuring 2 metres in height, the *Regalo di Canto* floor lamp is based on a series of moveable rotary-moulded polyethylene shells. Instead of a fixed object in a room, the light was designed for the observer to shape the piece. Both the colour and the intensity of the light changes as a result of its connection to a programmed computer. Apart from its function as a light source, it creates a meditative quality in a room, providing a gentle pulse-like radiance.

Regalo di Canto, which translates to 'gift of song', was designed to either soothe or energise a room. 'The shells in the light might be programmed to be more activated in a night club than in someone's own living area. It's the speed of the cycle that brings ambience to the space, whether it's the living or sleeping area,' he says. While one sculptural light creates a new song, arranging several lamps together creates a visual chorus.

SCHAMBURG + ALVISSE – A NEW FORM OF LIGHTING

144

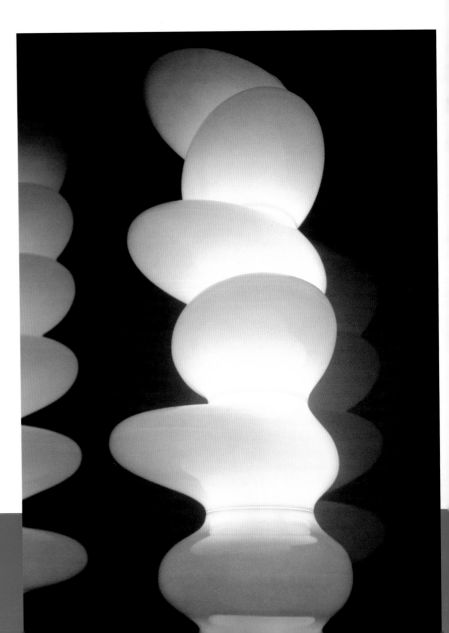

145

graphic design

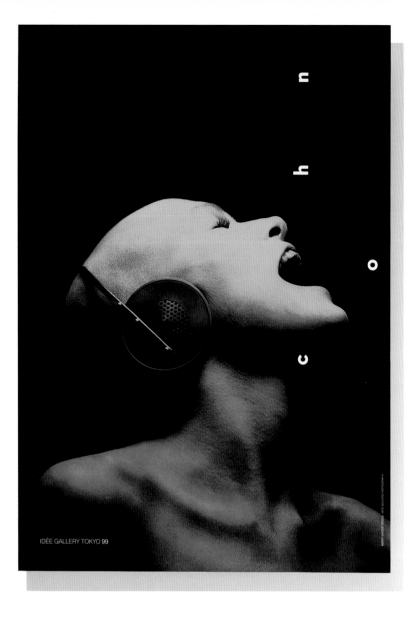

echo

IDÉE GALLERY TOKYO 99

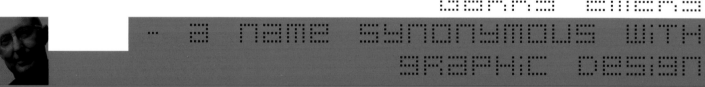

GARRY EMERY
... a name synonymous with graphic design

When it comes to graphic design, Garry Emery occupies centre stage among the major industry figures in Australia. With decades of experience and numerous awards, it is not surprising that a recent book on the remarkable design firm, Emery Vincent Design, sold out within weeks of its release.

Emery's designs encompass corporate brand identity, corporate communications, environmental graphic design and interactive media. 'The essence of a designer's hard core is a real desire to communicate, to explain, to teach and most importantly, to reveal. It's about exposing ideas through design so that the

readers or the viewers themselves "invent" or develop the meaning of the work. In the process, they themselves become designers for that moment,' Emery says.

Emery has developed an international profile as a result of projects overseas, but the name can also be identified closer to home with work on the Melbourne Exhibition Centre. Working with architects Denton Corker Marshall, graphics were developed that are as strong as the building's architectural lines.

Even though each brief is approached with a different strategy, some recurring techniques have helped to form the Emery signature. 'We frequently use the disruptive idea as a graphic tactic, putting people or objects into an unfamiliar context,' Emery says. With the catalogue for

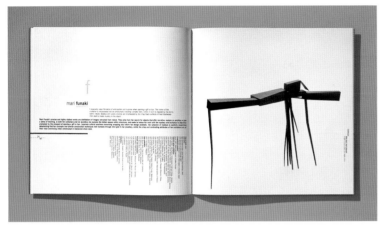

designer Susan Cohn, people wearing Cohn's jewellery were photographed on their sides. 'The images might be a little unfamiliar or even disturbing at times, but the images engage the viewer'.

One of the largest projects for Emery Vincent Design was the recent completion of the Kuala Lumpur City Centre. 'The scale of the work is obviously one of the issues. However, just as important is the cultural difference and the research that's required,' he says. For Emery Vincent Design, the use of computers over the last few years has allowed text and images to merge. As Emery says, 'Text has become pictorial. Now it's also about the new media and interactive media with direct communications'.

Garry Emery now heads Melbourne firm Garry Emery Design.

149

150

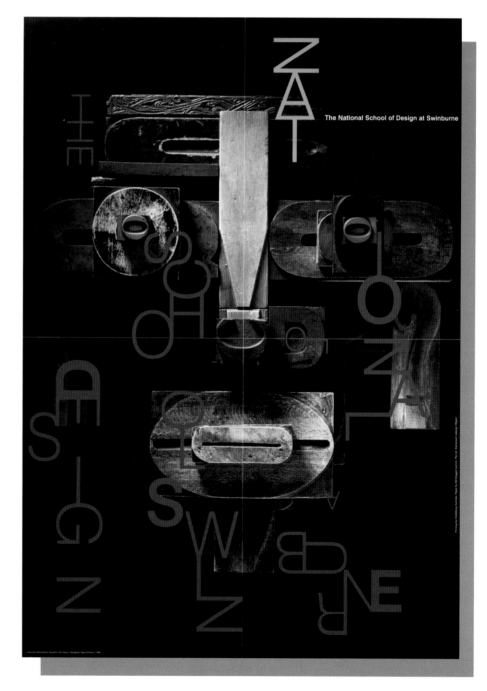

The National School of Design at Swinburne

151

153

With the flood of information and images that surround us on a daily basis, it's refreshing to hear graphic designer Brian Sadgrove's approach to design. 'My personal approach to design is to find the most simple and eloquent way to express an idea'. Like artists such as Matisse, the simplicity of the lines in Sadgrove's work are firmly embedded in one's mind.

The logo for Yarra Valley Water is simply defined by a single leaf and curvaceous line that suggests a running stream. Together, the two forms imply the purity of the water which is carried through the Victorian State Forest. Likewise, a logo designed for the City of Melbourne's Royal Botanic Gardens captures the wind

rustling through the majestic gardens. The colour of the autumn leaves and the verdant rolling lawns are swept through the image. 'There seems to be so much of everything. It's nice to be a reductionist, to do as much as possible with as little as possible. To edit and focus design resolutions so that in their own way, they are eloquent and not a victim of fashion,' Sadgrove says.

Unlike victims of fashion, which tend to come and go in the industry, Sadgrove is a pioneer in the field, commencing his own practice in 1968. The practice, which covers corporate and brand identity, packaging, editorial and architectural graphics and web site design succeeds in being able to get the message across with clarity and a sense of practicality. 'The best thing a potential client can say is, "I saw the job you did for so and so. Now I have this problem ..." or "I've heard you're good at ...",' Sadgrove says.

 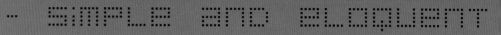

BRIAN SADGROVE - SIMPLE AND ELOQUENT

154

mayne

**ARTS
VICTORIA**

r o o s t

SPLITROCK

For Sadgrove, who often thought of becoming an architect, the built world holds a continual fascination, as does the interplay between space and form. The logo he designed for Arts Victoria demonstrates a fine juxtaposition of styles. The fluid lines of the implied flag for this logo creates a contrast to the strong and bold typography of the organisation.

As we continue to be inundated with images, Sadgrove's simple and eloquent images will remain embedded in our minds.

CINEMA

NOVA

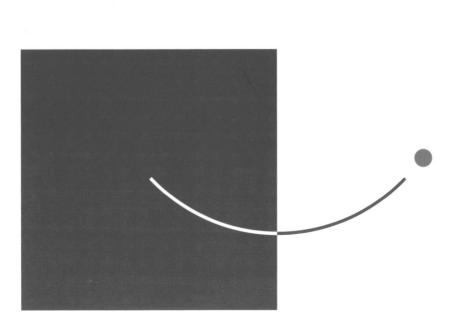

Ken Cato - a recognised language

As captivating as many of the dramas on Channel 7, Ken Cato's logo for the television station is a welcome break between shows. 'The introduction of colour transmission in 1975 prompted the Seven Network to utilise the colour bar as a recognisable and positive identity. The association with the colour red has always successfully conveyed a strong and dynamic message,' Cato says.

Ken Cato, who is synonymous with graphic design in Australia and has a large international following, was one of the first practices to turn the spotlight on graphic design. With a thirty-year history in the field, his projects and the mediums covered by the firm are extensive. For a campaign to celebrate the 70th anniversary of David Jones, one of Australia's leading department stores, the building was wrapped as if it were a giant present. Images from seven decades of women's fashion surfaced from every window of the historic sandstone building.

Whether the brief is for a corporation, an institution, or a business, the search for a powerful identity has become one of the single most important factors in achieving a strong marketplace presence. 'World markets are cluttered with organisations, products, entertainment and electronic services. There's all sorts of information that demands our attention. Our tolerance for pursuing anything that is not considered vitally important is almost non-existent,' Cato says.

energising the new economy

158

Even though we're surrounded by a flood of information, there is what Cato refers to as a Broader Visual Language. 'The Broader Visual Language is a graphics system that allows a corporation, business, brand or organisation to communicate successfully at all times, and therefore gain maximum marketplace presence,' Cato says. 'In the future, it's only those designers whose work is driven by ideas, who communicate with understanding and have a vision for Broader Visual Language, that will survive in the business arena,' he says.

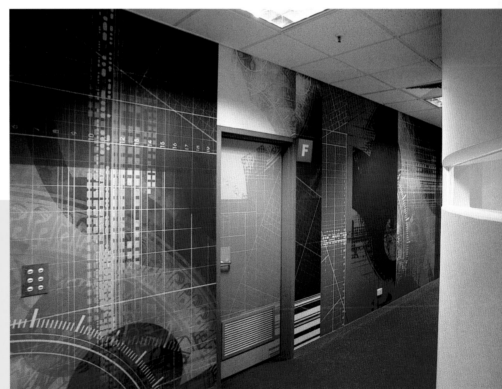

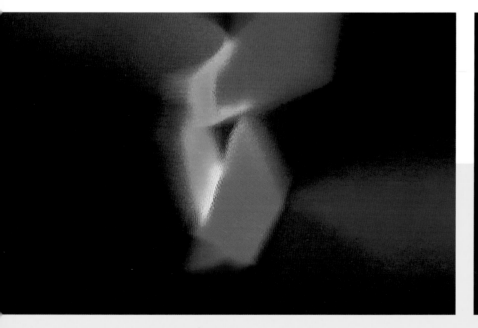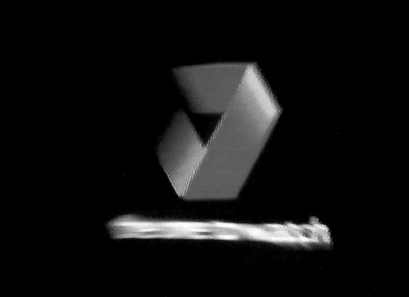

Short Films at...

MOONLIGHT CINEMA

CORNWELL – a sense of clarity

When Steven Cornwell and Jane Sinclair graduated in graphic design, they were eager to start their own practice. After a few years of working apart, Sinclair for a large firm and Cornwell freelancing on his own, the two joined forces. 'My first project was for Daryl Jackson [a leading Melbourne architect]. I worked on posters, brochures and books. I learnt a lot about the importance of communication and the skills required to clearly present ideas,' Cornwell says.

With the diversity of work that now comes through the studio – from brand identity, packaging and environmental design to interiors for institutional and corporate bodies – defining that certain style is difficult. 'I don't think that we have a certain style. It's more an approach to our work and providing a clarity that's understood by everyone. With the typography that we use, it's clear. We avoid the tricky fonts,' Cornwell says.

For the McClelland Gallery, which is a simple modernist building designed in the 1960s, the identity program devised by Cornwell was restrained. 'This building is sunk into the landscape and has an international modernist feel. When you look at the signage for some of the great museums, such as the Guggenheim in New York, it's also simple and played-down,' he says.

In contrast to the restraint shown for the McClelland Gallery, the campaign Cornwell designed for the Moonlight Cinema has a strong humorous side. 'We observed the type of people who were attending the cinema over a period of time. The crowd had a slightly nerdy feel, but smart and intellectual,' Cornwell says. The words 'Moonlight Cinema' literally dance between the man's thick-rimmed glasses and his retro-style hat.

For the Sir William Angliss Centre, a training institution for the hospitality industry, the glass façade of the building designed by Woods Bagot Architects allowed Cornwell to go beyond the 'lifestyle' approach to food. 'You can see the murals through the glass façades. It was an opportunity to bring the name out to the streets'. When it came to designing the graphics and the interior for PTO (in conjunction with Bates Smart Architects), the client used the term 'retailment', something that went beyond a store that simply sold products. Aimed at the 14–25-year-old market, the pink and fuschia palette has a cheeky, girlish ambience. 'There's a chat room and you can also buy CDs. It's like going over to your girlfriend's house'.

While the approach differs for every project, there is always a sense of clarity. As Cornwell says, 'We don't like to be distracted. The work needs to be the focus. It's a matter of communicating the ideas clearly and finding the right approach'.

165

welcome to the future.

caring. a genuine concern about client needs / problem solving and providing support at all stages of a client's project.

confident. confidence to make recommendations, confidence in the product, confidence to develop ongoing client relationships and confidence in delivery.

capable. capable in delivery, expertise, creation and management.

modern. by constantly evaluating products, maintaining relevance and staying one step ahead of our competitors we are a truly modern organisation / making the successful transition from old to new services to Edwards Dunlop is an organisation in touch with the future.

practical. sensitive to the environment needs and realities / not only promoting, yet providing realistic, delivery schedules, understanding the digital environment or providing practical solutions.

edwards dunlop paper

When designers Fabio Ongarato and Ronnen Goren came together in the early 1990s, graphic design wasn't the only connection. 'We had the same interests, from architecture to fashion,' Ongarato says. Goren, who studied architecture at RMIT, briefly worked in his profession before heading down the museum and exhibition track. Ongarato, however, was keen to set up his own design studio, after graduating from the same university in visual communications.

The practice, which is multi-disciplinary and includes staff designers from all over the world, takes its lead from practices such as the Eames Office in California. 'We're not thinking in post-war terms. What we appreciated about the Eames office was their enormous interest in a range of design areas. They were continually experimenting with a variety of things, turning the ordinary into the extraordinary,' Goren says. While each brief takes a different format, there is a certain manner in which the task of designing is approached. 'We generally start the process by asking ourselves, "What are we trying to say?" It's a matter of starting from scratch with the pen and paper. Down the track, we then bring in people from a number of disciplines, from photographers to artists,' Ongarato says.

168

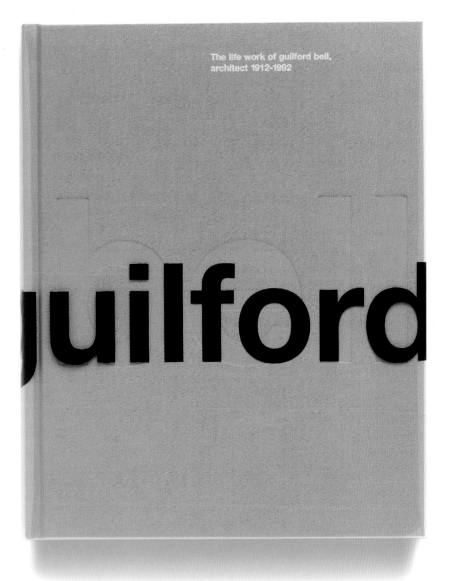

The life work of guilford bell, architect 1912-1992

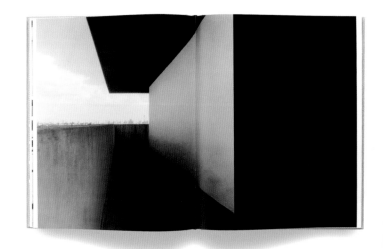

For the Melbourne Fashion Festival, the images of the models were blurred and portrayed an energy. Instead of a single model facing the audience, the graphics capture the movement and feeling of the event. 'It was really about stripping away the glamour of the event and conveying the dynamics of the show,' Ongarato says. For the Australian fashion label Scanlan & Theodore, the tightly cropped eye with long eye lashes beckons the viewer's attention, as does the model who halts us in our tracks. The power of the imagery stems partly from the knowledge and research for each brief. A book on the legendary Australian architect Guilford Bell goes well beyond a composition in greys, showing a closer understanding of the architect's work. 'Bell had a strict sense of symmetry. His buildings were elegant and he showed a real sense of control over his craft,' Goren says. A sense of elegance and control can also be seen in the work of Fabio Ongarato.

BRIGHT AND SHINING オーストラリアの輝き

ARTISTS: TIM JOHNSON, LINDY LEE, VICTORIA LOBREGAT, NATSUHO TAKITA CURATED BY MELISSA CHIU

OXFORD

SPRING

00/01

POINT, LIFE, LINE

'A line is the shortest distance of one point for another.
The shortest path.'

7.1 musings

An museum at the century's turn have become new kinds of public institutions. They are very different from their original form, when collecting was a more private activity of accumulation, of guarding the present (and past) against ravaging time or through their subsequent evolution to be understood as the functional housing of specific collections. In their recently expanded domain, they are increasingly devoted to public education, of both art history and of emerging forms of contemporary art, actively encouraging reflection, enquiry and knowledge at the same time as providing enjoyment.

Museums and galleries are also being required to fill another role, increasingly being deployed as primary catalysts for urban regeneration or as landmarks in redefining a city's identity. These potential effects now far exceed simple use or utility. In this process, distinctive architecture has been widely used as the key component in staging the contemporary museum as an event in its own right. Museums are becoming recognised as much, if not more, through their power as iconic buildings as they are through their collections.

There is however a shadowing disquiet, where the museum building as an event utterly overwhelms the art it contains as the subject of attention. It is one instance in which cultural tourism has become more important as a presentation than the actual experience of art. Creating new conditions for the experience of art as a different enterprise to violating what already exists, or in the museum serving as an event

Jahn, E, 1994, *The Book of Lineage*, V:7.1, Winslyre University Press.

Peter Davidson graduated in 1980 from the NSW Institute of Technology in Sydney. After arriving in London in 1981 he was appointed editorial assistant on the journal *International Architect*. He ran his own practice for ten years whilst simultaneously teaching at a number of institutions, including the Architectural Association (AA) and Bartlett School of Architecture, and was a visiting critic at many others. In addition, Peter was co-partner in several well-known projects at the AA. Peter is co-founder, principal of Lab architecture studio and currently working on their winning competition proposal for Federation Square, Melbourne.

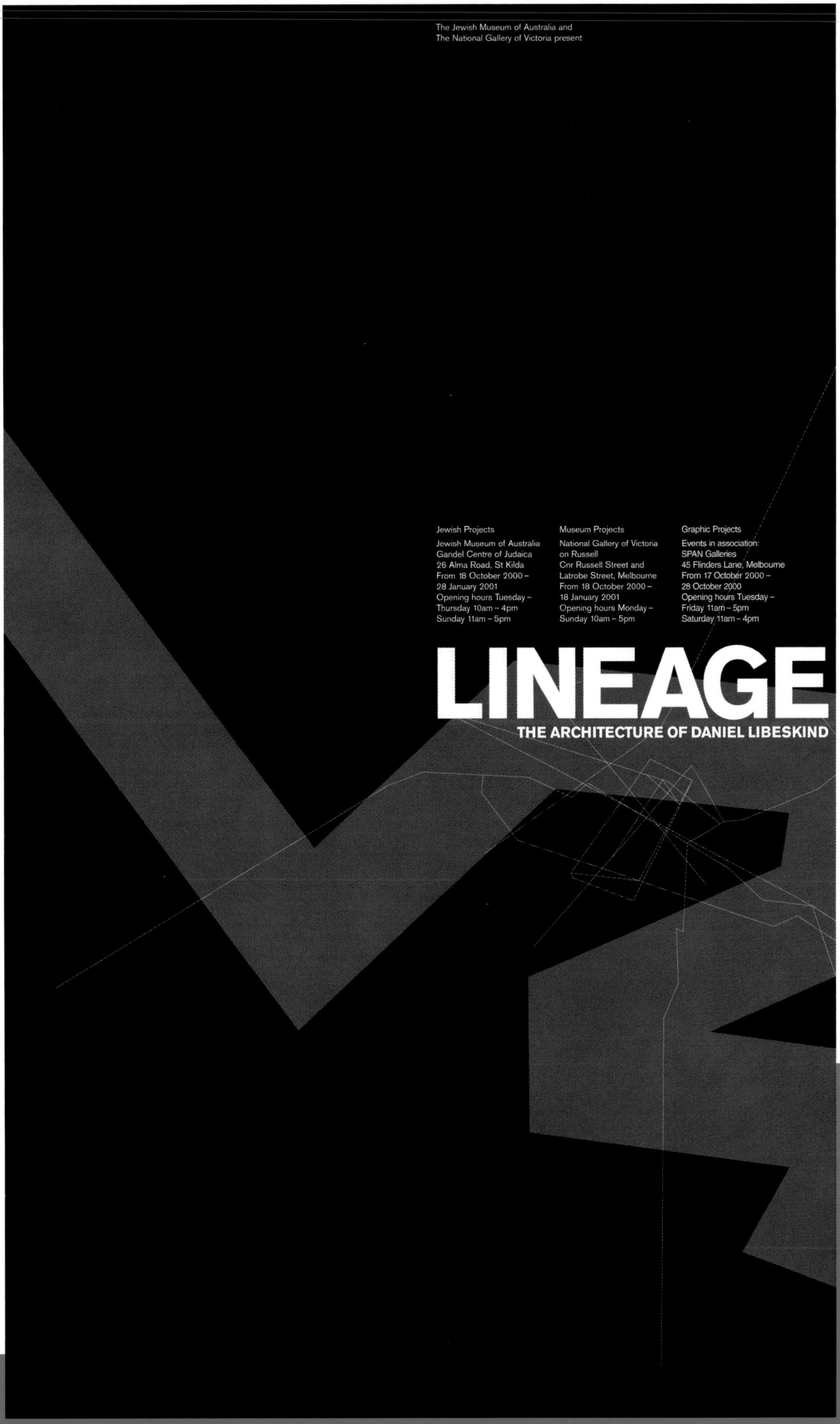

The Jewish Museum of Australia and
The National Gallery of Victoria present

Jewish Projects
Jewish Museum of Australia
Gandel Centre of Judaica
26 Alma Road, St Kilda
From 18 October 2000 –
28 January 2001
Opening hours Tuesday –
Thursday 10am – 4pm
Sunday 11am – 5pm

Museum Projects
National Gallery of Victoria
on Russell
Cnr Russell Street and
Latrobe Street, Melbourne
From 18 October 2000 –
18 January 2001
Opening hours Monday –
Sunday 10am – 5pm

Graphic Projects
Events in association:
SPAN Galleries
45 Flinders Lane, Melbourne
From 17 October 2000 –
28 October 2000
Opening hours Tuesday –
Friday 11am – 5pm
Saturday 11am – 4pm

LINEAGE
THE ARCHITECTURE OF DANIEL LIBESKIND

04

thought.design

CREATING A STORM

When graphic design practice Storm first opened its doors 10 years ago, directors Dean Butler and David Ansett had only just closed the door on Prahran College, from which they had graduated. 'We really didn't want to work for anyone else. We were fairly naive to begin with, but we shared a passion for design,' Butler says.

One of the first large commissions for Storm was with the City of Stonnington in Melbourne, designing the corporate wardrobes and ancillary items such as notebooks and pens. Instead of prescribing conservative ties with small neat patterns, these were designed with a slightly 1970s retro feel. Likewise, the corporate scarves were photographed against a bright blue sky in a unique image. 'There are probably about 400 different items that are generated by Storm, from street signs to flags and banners. That work has led to other councils now using our services, across the Melbourne metropolitan area,' he says.

Over the last 10 years, Storm has seen a change in the way graphic design is approached. 'The focus is now on branding an organisation and developing an almost human personality around it. While it is highly intuitive in one sense, finding the right approach for an organisation also requires a rational and researched method. It's not just about the aesthetics of a project. Before we start work on any single project we establish a design strategy that is specific to the client, the personality of their product, their target audience, the direction and history of their company and its position within the market that they operate,' says Butler.

Ironically, as a result of varied commissions, defining Storm's signature is a most difficult task. The Hemisphere Clothing Company, for example,

177

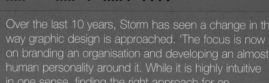

was defined by four images on its swing tag. 'The lion represents masculinity, the second is the letter H for Hemisphere, the third emblem is a fleur de lys for the owner's Italian heritage, while the fourth is a hand with a heart embossed on it. The last image represents the love that they put into their designs and gives their range of clothing a hand-made quality'.

While branding is now an integral part of the Storm practice, the future is also in the management side to the branding process. 'It's a matter of making sure the images are used and placed to the greatest effect. You are literally bombarded with images out there and so we need to make sure that our images are consistent and highly focused,' Butler says. With a string of awards, this vibrant practice continues to take the market by storm.

178

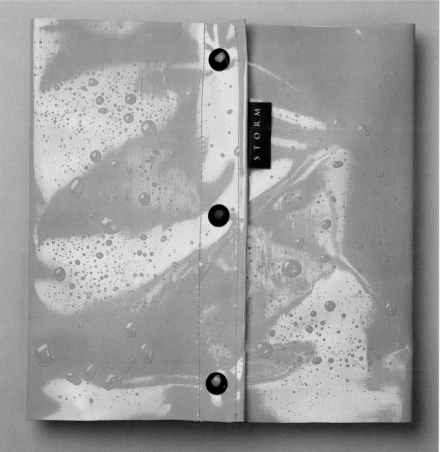

179

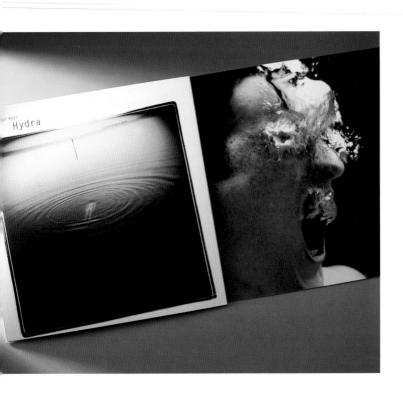

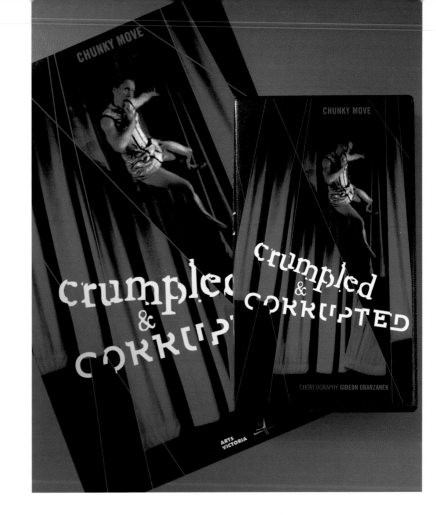

Graphic design firm Asprey Di Donato Design began in the late 1980s, and the process of discovery and learning was inherent from day one. 'What we found very early on was that it was up to us to educate our clients and make them understand the role of design. It was fairly challenging as it made us ask questions about design and its role before we could successfully sell design,' Tony Di Donato, one of the directors of the firm says.

More than ten years later, Tony Di Donato and his partner Peter Asprey continue to sell design, discovering new things about themselves and their clients in the process. 'Whether we are developing a new brand for ice cream or developing a corporate identity for a state government, we search for an insight. That insight could be consumer-driven, but it's this insight that we then get to work with,' Di Donato says. For two programs for dance company Chunky Moves, *Hydra* and *Crumpled and Corrupted*, we had to communicate the energy of the performances. In keeping with the company's energetic and diverse choreography, the water used for

Hydra shows the two sides of the company. Simple lines form in the still water like the result of throwing a stone. The image is sharply contrasted with the power of water against a dancer's face.

Asprey Di Donato's design for Anzac Biscuits goes beyond trying to capture the appeal or taste of the biscuit. 'The design was to capture a authentic feel for the Anzac biscuit. As it isn't an original recipe, it was important for the packaging to capture an historic feel,' Di Donato says. To gain a holistic approach to their work, Asprey Di Donato recently formed an alliance

181

with Massive Interactive (New Media) and Nonstop Partners (Innovation Team) to form an exciting collective, registered as SOUP. 'This model brings together people from various disciplines, ranging from strategic planners, a food technologist, and researchers to creative teams, in a journey of consumer discovery,' he says.

Whether the project is a credentials document, displaying the State of Victoria's point of difference, or creating the designs for a beverage company, there is extensive research behind each design which often fades behind the image created.

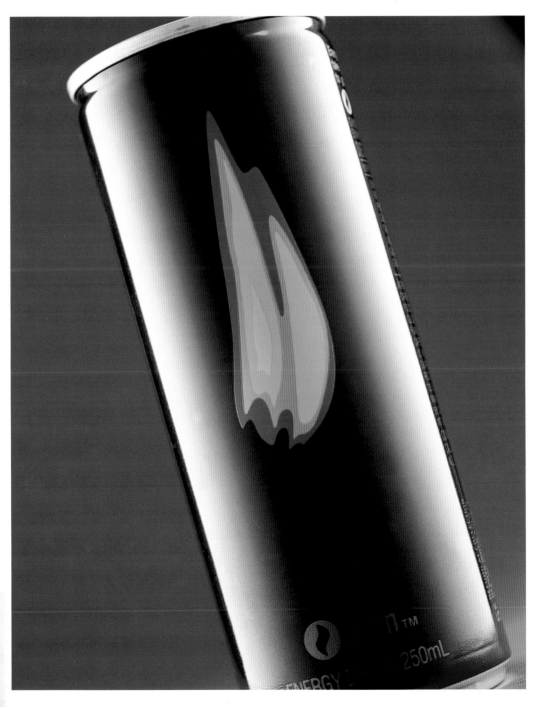

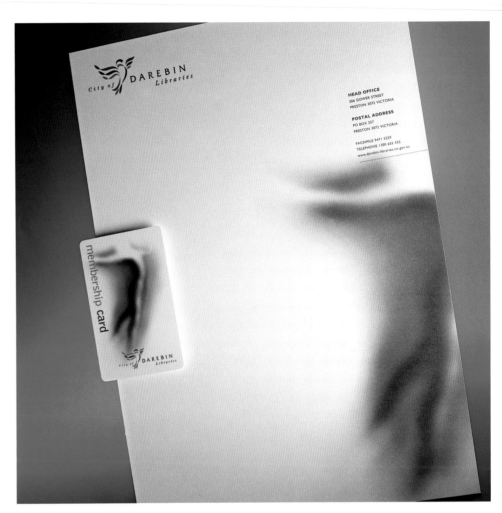

photography

The name John Gollings has become synonymous with photography, particularly architectural photography. It comes as no surprise that Gollings studied architecture at The University of Melbourne, before deciding on a career in photography.

Images of a new home featuring the actress Pamela Anderson on its façade, create an indelible mark on the viewer. Likewise, a city footbridge takes on a heroic form. Even when the subject is a woman simply gazing out of a window while sipping a cappuccino, her thoughts appear to be visible to the viewer. An advertisement for hosiery not only conveys the comfort of the product, but the pleasure that's derived from

wearing it. A simple staircase or an open door gives the subject a new dimension as the eye wanders into the unchartered territory. The silhouette of Gollings in the foreground on one assignment is as intriguing as the building itself.

With undue modesty, Gollings simplifies his approach to photography. 'My photography is obsessively based on a rigorous compositional cross. Clarity and legibility are paramount. Objects are shot on plain black, white or grey backgrounds. The buildings are generally shot front on and centred in the view finder. I photograph people as if they were buildings, mid-point and with the correct perspective,' he says.

JOHN GOLLINGS - ICONIC PHOTOGRAPHY

190

191

While not articulated every time he stands behind a camera, Gollings has certain rules that guide his work. 'I like design to have an idea. I appreciate fine, legible topography while I hate overprinting, coloured papers or background printing. Pictures should sit in their own space'.

Despite the accolades for Gollings both in Australia and internationally, resting on his laurels is not on the current agenda. 'I would expect my work to be "edgy", to go beyond the expected, or better than expected, and to challenge accepted norms of style and taste,' Gollings says. This edgy feel is delivered with the technical resources and craftsmanship of a true professional.

193

newaustraliaSTYLE

For Hyatt, who travels around Australia capturing the finest architecture in the country on film, there is always a story behind the image. 'I saw images in my childhood, often simple images like cartoons or clippings of poems that I formed into a scrap book. I certainly wasn't craving to be an architect,' Hyatt says. Hyatt, who worked as a photo journalist with *The Age* for a number of years, is acutely aware of the story as well as the image for each assignment.

Whether the image is of a building designed by Japanese architect Kengo Kuma or the work of celebrated Australian architect Glenn Murcutt, there is a genuine honesty about Hyatt's photography and the buildings conveyed in them. 'I strive to identify a project's quintessential qualities. I analyse its strengths and weaknesses and the result is somewhere between deer stalker and scientist. I tend to work intuitively and systematically, whether I shoot a project or a portrait,' Hyatt says.

Unlike many photographers who focus their attention only on the image, Hyatt also writes extensively, together with making documentaries. Hyatt's documentary on Glenn Murcutt, *Touch this Earth Lightly*, shows the same sensitivity in celluloid as the architect does for the Australian landscape. 'Sometimes it is difficult wearing so many hats. One moment you have to present yourself as a writer or photographer or both, at other times it's being a film video maker,' he says.

196

Peter Hyatt

Gabriel **Poole**
John **Mainwaring**
Lindsay and Kerry **Clare**

LOCAL**HEROES**

Architects of Australia's Sunshine Coast

FULL COLOUR SATURATION

A few houses away from Andrew Metcalf's latest residential project in Clontarf, Sydney, sits a house reputedly designed by an architect who had also worked as a Luftwaffe pilot. Such irony of circumstance. It's a piece of pure modernist austerity. Its roof-top "playground" and masonry and glass form clearly pays tribute to Le Corbusier's classic, Villa Savoie outside of Paris.

This derivative is an imposing cone of structure which by virtue of its sheer size and bulk parodies the very philosophy of reduction implicit in such a genre. Just up the hill is the new kid on the block. It stands as if to prove the point how design references, when ably recycled and manipulated, can produce intriguing and robust variations upon the theme.

Taking the Rubik's Cube of primary colours and possibilities, the Arnold House is like a hologram created by a high-tech Piet Mondrian. It has an irresistible presence with its vividly painted steel work, yet its luminosity captures a light, ethereal quality. Here illustration becomes structure and structure illustrated.

Hyatt's book *Local Heroes, Architects of Australia's Sunshine Coast* is as edgy and light-filled as the coastal architecture that is photographed. While Hyatt doesn't claim to redefine a building, he does bring out its most salient features. 'I have a maxim for photographing buildings. Basically it says that with a camera, you can elevate everything a notch. A bad building can be made to look okay, an okay building can be made to look very good and a very good building becomes sensational,' Hyatt says.

While the Atami Villa by Kengo Kuma is a sensational building, it becomes truly memorable set against the ocean views. Great photography is about putting together such distinctive elements in a unified way.

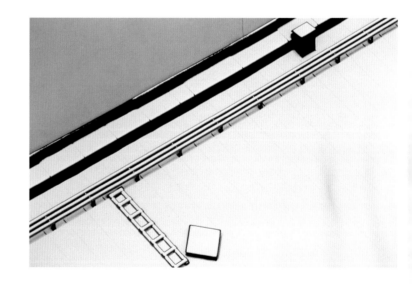

TREVOR MEIN – CAPTURING THE LAYERS

With a diploma in fashion design and a Bachelor of Architecture, it's not surprising that photographer Trevor Mein came to photography with an eye for his subject matter. Architecture isn't just a form or conglomeration of materials, but many subtle layers. 'It was only late in my career that people referred to my work as layered. Often they remark that I manage to capture the complexity of the design,' Mein says.

The office of architects Neil & Idle, a landmark building in the Melbourne suburb of Richmond, suggested, among other things, a shield, from both the viewers

eagerly trying to look in and the occupants gazing over the neighbouring rooftops. 'The building has an industrial quality. However, it appears as a veil that's quite sheer,' Mein says. Instead of trying to capture the more industrial edge to the building, Mein presented the softer, more feminine qualities of the design. When it came to photographing H_2O's design for RMIT's Brunswick Campus, the brief was to capture more than an unusual façade. 'With the light, the building changes its form at different times of the day. I wanted to present a deeply modulated design that has been finely wrapped for the pleasure of the occupants,' he says.

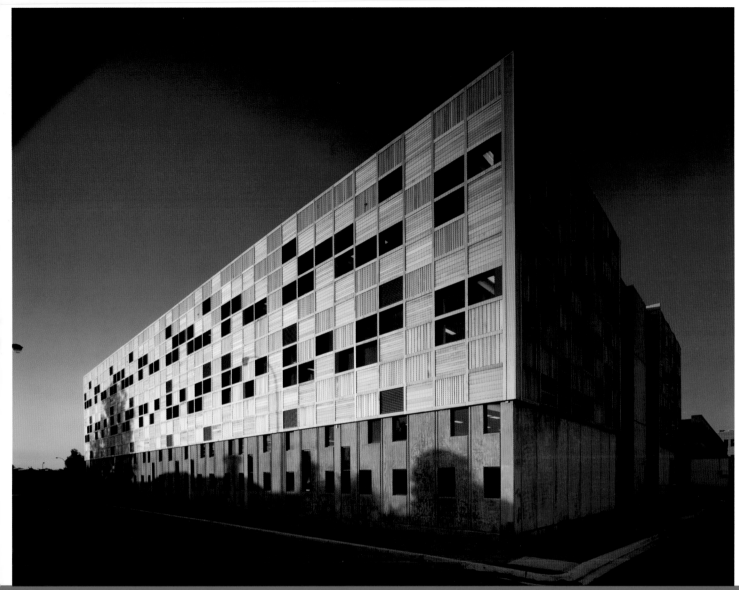

A beach house, designed by architect Nik Karalis of Woods Bagot, was photographed by Mein displaying the extreme beauty of both the building and the landscape. A glass façade, which acts as a mirror to reflect the clouds and the sand dunes, captures the extremes of the design. 'It's quite a brutalist type of screen, but the reflections give it a delicacy'. For an image of an award-winning design by architects Field Consultants, the strength of the architecture is rivalled by the powerful limbs of an established oak tree.

The information about a building is as important to architectural photography as the light conditions on the day. 'I'm conscious of the space, the volume, the scale, the materials and the relationship that they form with the physical environment. I try and define the strengths of a building and in my mind the most demanding viewer is standing over my shoulder. Whether it's a complex building or a more simple form, I would hope that my images trigger an interest for those wanting to seek out the original,' Mein says.

205

GREG BARRETT — A NEW ANGLE

Photographer Greg Barrett is often defined by the energetic ballet figures he captures on film. His dancers soar through spaces or find themselves placed in extraordinary positions. In Barrett's book *Tutu*, the dancers Rachel Dougherty and Joshua Consandine seem to defy gravity. Likewise, the agility of Bradley Chatfield was unbounded when he was published in the book *Danceshots*.

'When I'm photographing dancers I'm not only trying to capture the moment which ends up on the page, I'm also trying to suggest the moments before and after the event, which must be drawn out of the viewer's imagination,' Barrett says.

For Barrett, whether the subject is a dancer, a shadow on the pavement, a baby's face, the sunlight on a girl's neck or a simple object such as a bottle of Coca Cola, 'It's a matter of making something fresh that will excite the eye,' he says. The strength of women such as the late Mietta O'Donnell (the renowned restaurateur) and Nancy Pilcher (Editor-in-Chief of *Vogue Australia*) doesn't require an elaborate setting to give them a voice. As Barrett says, 'It takes some collaboration with the viewer to make the image complete itself'.

For portraits of the musicians Helena Rathbone and Yi Wang of the Australian Chamber Orchestra, Barrett instils a surrealistic quality. The large double bass,

which acts as Wang's reflection, shows the dedication of these talented artists. 'I was trying to show how I felt to be in the same room as these hugely gifted and dedicated people. The portraits have a likeness, but you wouldn't necessarily be able to identify them if they walked into the same room,' Barrett says.

Even a self-portrait shot by Barrett takes on a third dimension. Barrett's photographic eye draws in the viewer, as do the rhythmic geometric shapes that frame his torso. As Barrett says, 'I'm always looking for the shape, which is the essence of that thing I've concentrated on. The image slips into your mind and, for a time, makes its home there'.

212

Daniel MacDougall's black and white images are hauntingly beautiful. Segmented playing cards are carefully arranged next to Edwardian-style tie pins encrusted with pearls. Another image shows a wedding photo framed with a few personal possessions. The images, which have an inner light, are a fitting tribute to the photographer's grandfather, pianist Stanley Arthur Rogers.

MacDougall started working as a photographic assistant before studying photography at RMIT. 'I try to approach my work conceptually and build the images up to convey a feeling,' he says. For MacDougall, the collection of photographs titled *La Ondaj*, translated as *The Waves*, was designed as a tribute to his grandfather. 'My grandfather was very well-read and his favourite author was Virginia Wolfe. He was fond of the whole Bloomsbury group,' he says. When his grandfather passed away, MacDougall sorted through his belongings. 'They might appear as simple objects that have just been arranged for an effect. However, each set of objects says something about what my grandfather thought about simple things where he lived'. A set of feathers that has been firmly bound sits lightly on a set of silver spoons. 'Even though my grandfather might not have been a

DANIEL MACDOUGALL
- TREASURED MEMORIES

213

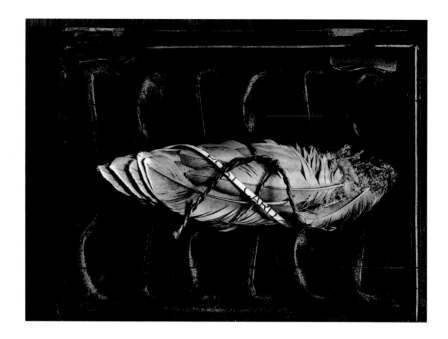

worldly traveller, he still could enjoy the finer things that life could offer'. The numbers two and three regularly appear in the photos, recalling the number 23, the number of the house where he lived.

An image of two spoons joined together, like a crucifix, recalls Roger's admiration for women. 'I think that he felt that females were more in control than males. He also had a strong feminine side to his personality,'

MacDougall says. The series of images can be likened to a series of portraits, each one carefully revealing something new about the man. For MacDougall, capturing the images in black and white allows a greater degree of manipulation. 'I can create more light and shade. I tend to make the prints quite dark and heavy and then I bleach away the areas that I want to highlight. I prefer using colour, particularly rich bold colours, for my commercial work'.

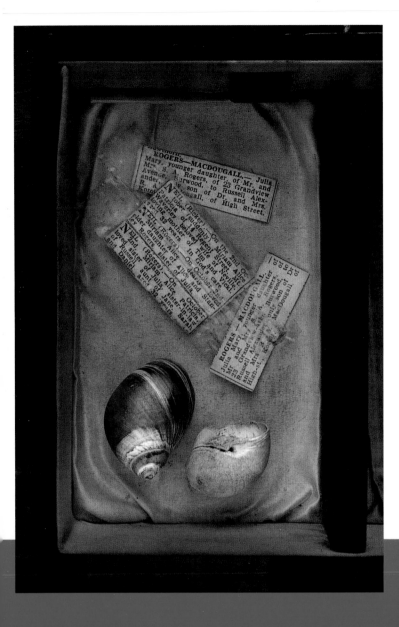

When photographer Andrew Curtis saw David Lynch's film *Eraserhead* as a teenager, his focus was set. '*Eraserhead* had a surreal quality about it. The film was dark and mysterious. Architecture and objects were transformed into surrealistic landscapes,' Curtis says.

More than twenty years on and well-established in his profession, Curtis hasn't swayed from the childhood recollections. A fertiliser factory, usually screened from the public gaze, takes on the form of a heroic mountainous landscape in his images. Likewise, substations and machinery used for tooling are

heightened to an art form. When the machinery is presented in the usual catalogue format, the images are mundane and lifeless. However, in Curtis' mind, the humble machines take on a human quality. The excess oil which oozes from the machines takes on the appearance of blood. Likewise, the various tubes that Curtis arranges in the machine's orifices have sexual connotations. Other machines from the ESP factory, titled *ESP Machinery* [images four and five], have either a bird-like form or can be read as a chomping mouth.

When Curtis became intrigued with electrical substations, surrounded by barbed-wire fences, the image of a trapped animal played on his mind. 'For years I was thinking of the best possible way to photograph these substations, trying to remove the thorny foregrounds. However, the wire is really part of the story. The effect is like beasts that have been caged,' Curtis says. *Deepdene 3* isn't just another substation, but is animated. 'It's like a proud giraffe that's looking out towards the viewer,' he says.

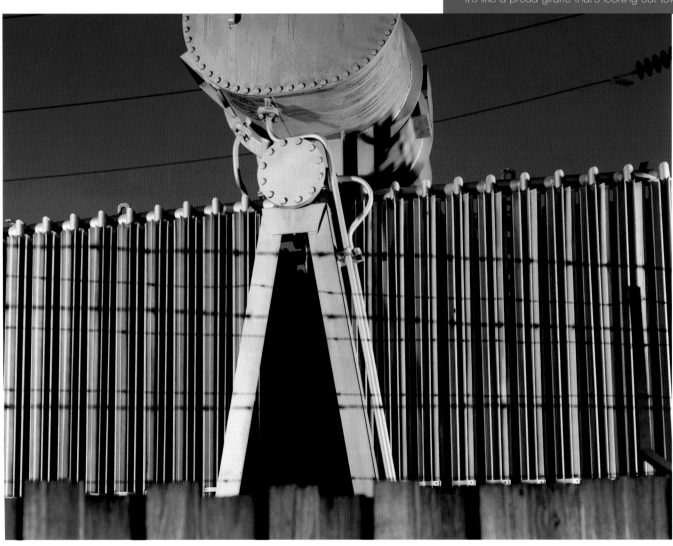

More recently, Curtis has found inspiration in the simple building sites around him. However, unlike many architectural photographers who celebrate the built form, Curtis centres his attention on the foundations and the rubble on the site. 'These forms are my raw materials. I love transforming them into surrealist objects or situations'. Like artists such as Van Gogh, who painted the starry night as a crazy, swirling sky, the simple machinery seized upon by Curtis takes on heroic proportions.

'I tend to light the machines to create drama and isolate the machine in its own world. The rest of the factory and the machines are left in darkness,' he says. The images might be considered disturbing for some, however, once caught on film, the machinery is transformed into objects of both sculptural and photographic integrity.

Jewellery Susan Cohn Page 12: Earl Carter, Iasmu Sawa; Page 13: John Gollings; Page 14: Earl Carter, John Gollings, Kate Gollings; Page 15: Earl Carter; Portrait: Kate Gollings **Mari Funaki** Page 16: Terence Bogue; Page 17: Terence Bogue; Page 18: Terence Bogue; Page 19: Sally Marsland, Terence Bogue; Portrait: courtesy of Mari Funaki **Marian Hosking** Page 20: Danielle Thompson; Page 21: Danielle Thompson; Page 22: Danielle Thompson; Portrait: courtesy Marian Hosking **Dinosaur Designs** Page 23: Ashley Barber; Page 24: Ashley Barber; Page 25: Ashley Barber; Page 26: Ashley Barber; Portrait: courtesy Dinosaur Designs **Warwick Freeman** Page 27: Patrick Reynolds; Page 28: Patrick Reynolds; Page 29: Patrick Reynolds; Page 30: Patrick Reynolds; Portrait: Patrick Reynolds **Alan Preston** Page 31: Julia Brook; Page 32: Julie Brook; Page 33: Julie Brook; Page 34: Julia Brook; Page 35: Julia Brook; Portrait: Vicky Hamill

Ceramics, Glass and Metal Fink and Co. Page 38: Damien McDonald; Page 39: Damien McDonald; Page 40: Damien McDonald; Page 41: Russell Pell, Robert Foster; Page 42: Damien McDonald, Penny Boyer; Page 43: Penny Boyer; Portrait: Robert Foster **Simon Lloyd** Page 44: Terence Bogue; Page 45: Terence Bogue; Page 46: Terence Bogue; Page 47: Terence Bogue; Portrait: Terence Bogue **Stephane P. Rondel** Page 48: Dario Grassi; Page 49: Dario Grassi, Haru Sameshima; Page 50: Dario Grassi; Portrait: Claude Lapeyere **Maureen Williams** Page 51: Robert Colvin, Terence Bogue; Page 52: Peter Budd, Terence Bogue; Page 53: Robert Colvin, Terence Bogue; Page 54: Robert Colvin, Terence Bogue, David McArthur; Portrait: courtesy of Maureen Williams **Robert Knottenbelt** Page 55: Robert Colvin, Terence Bogue; Page 56: Robert Colvin; Page 57: Robert Colvin; Portrait: courtesy Robert Knottenbelt

Sculpture Geoffrey Bartlett Page 60: Geoffrey Bartlett; Page 61: John Gollings; Page 62: John Gollings, Geoffrey Bartlett; Page 63: John Gollings; Page 64: John Gollings; Page 65: Geoffrey Bartlett; Page 66: Geoffrey Bartlett, John Gollings; Portrait: courtesy of Geoffrey Bartlett **Peter D. Cole** Page 67: John Brash; Page 68: John Brash; Page 69: John Brash; Portrait: John Brash **Inge King** Page 70: Grahame King; Page 71: Grahame King; Page 72: Grahame King; Portrait: Grahame King **Augustine Dall'Ava** Page 73: Vicki Petherbridge; Page 74: Vicki Petherbridge; Page 75: Vicki Petherbridge; Page 76: Vicki Petherbridge; Portrait: Vicki Petherbridge **Robert Bridgewater** Page 77: Ken Irwin; Page 78: Ken Irwin; Page 79: Ken Irwin; Page 80: Ken Irwin; Page 81: Ken Irwin; Portrait: Ken Irwin

Furniture Marc Newson Page 84: Marc Newson Ltd; Page 85: Marc Newson Ltd; Page 86: Marc Newson Ltd; Page 87: Marc Newson Ltd; Page 88: Marc Newson Ltd; Page 89: Marc Newson Ltd; Page 90: Marc Newson Ltd; Page 91: Marc Newson Ltd; Page 92: Tom Vack; Page 93: Marc Newson Ltd; Portrait: Karin Catt **MAP** Page: 94 Trevor Mein; Page 95: Trevor Mein; Page 96: Trevor Mein; Page 97: Trevor Mein; Portrait: courtesy MAP **join** Page 98: Trevor Mein; Page 99: Trevor Mein; Page 100: Trevor Mein; Page 101: Trevor Mein; Page 102: Trevor Mein; Page 103: Trevor Mein; Portrait: Isamu Sawa **Caroline Casey** Page 104: Jonathan Rose; Page 105: David Mist, Jonathan Rose; Page 106: David Mist; Page 107: David Mist; Page 108: Jonathan Rose; Portrait: Penelope Clay **Schamburg + Alvisse** Page 109: Alister Clarke; Page 110: John Webber; Page 111: Alister Clarke; Page 112: John Webber, Alister Clarke; Portrait: John Weber **Tim Miller** Page 113: Tim Miller; Page 114: Tim Miller; Page 115: Tim Miller; Portrait: Paul Hillier **David Trubridge** Page 116: Peter Tang, Haru Sameshima; Page 117: David Evans, Peter Tang; Page 118: Graeme Cornwell; Page 118: David Evans, Denys McNicholl, David Evans; Page 119: David Evans, David Trubridge; Portrait: courtesy of David Trubridge **Humphrey Ikin** Page 120: courtesy Humphrey Ikin; Page 121: courtesy Humphrey Ikin; Page 122: courtesy Humphrey Ikin; Page 123: courtesy Humphrey Ikin; Portrait: courtesy Humphrey Ikin

Lighting Denis Smitka Page 126: Shania Shegedyn, Terence Bogue; Page 127: Terence Bogue; Page 128: Shania Shegedyn; Page 129: Shania Shegedyn, Terence Bogue; Page 130: Shania Shegedyn, Terence Bogue; Portrait: courtesy of Denis Smitka **Ism Objects** Page 131: David Ascoli; Page 132: David Ascoli; Page 133: David Ascoli; Page 134: David Ascoli; Page 135: David Ascoli; Page 136: David Ascoli; Page 137: David Ascoli; Page 138: David Ascoli; Portrait: David Ascoli **Marc Pascal** Page: 139: Garth Oriander, Terence Bogue; Page 140: Terence Bogue; Page 141: Terence Bogue; Page 142: Terence Bogue; Page 143: Terence Bogue; Portrait: Narelle Wilson **Schamburg + Alvisse** Page 144: John Webber; Page 145: John Webber; Portrait: John Webber

Graphic Design Garry Emery Design Page 148: Earl Carter; Page 149: Earl Carter; Page 150: Earl Carter; Page 151: Earl Carter; Page 152: Earl Carter; Page 153: Earl Carter; Portrait Earl Carter **Brian Sadgrove** Page 154: courtesy Brain Sadgrove Design; Page 155: courtesy Brain Sadgrove Design ; Page 156: courtesy Brain Sadgrove Design; Portrait: courtesy Brain Sadgrove Design **Ken Cato** Page 157: Mark Rayner; Page 158: courtesy of Ken Cato Design; Page 159: Mark Rayner; Page 160: Mark Rayner; Page 161: Mark Rayner; Page 162: Mark Rayner and courtesy of Ken Cato Design; Portrait: courtesy of Ken Cato Design **Steven Cornwell** Page 163: photography/Illustration by Cornwell Design, Andrew Curtis; Page 164: Andrew Curtis, Trevor Mein; Page 165: commissioned by M+C Saatchi; Page 166: Con Nicolofski; Page 167: photography/illustration by Cornwell Design; Portrait: Trevor Mein **Fabio Ongarato** Page 168: Fiona McDonald; Page 169: Michele Aboud, Stephane Sednaoui; Page 170: Trevor Mein; Page 171: Trevor Mein; Page 172: courtesy Fabio Ongarato; Page 173: Derek Henderson; Page 176: courtesy Fabio Ongarato; Portrait: Trevor Mein **Storm** Page 177: Photomanifesto, Photographers; Page 176: Photomanifesto, Photographers; Page 177: Paul Monroe, Grassy Knoll, Photographers; Page 179: Photomanifesto, Photographers; Portrait: Photomanifesto, Photographers **Asprey Di Donato** Page 180: Sandy Nicholson, David Obarzanek, Chunky Moves, Garth Oriander; Page 181: Charles Stewart, Garth Oriander; Page 182: Show Ads, Earl Carter; Page 183: Illustrated by Sergio Medina and photographed by Garth Oriander; Page 184: Garth Oriander; Page 185: Garth Oriander, Jacqui Henshaw; Page 186: Earl Carter; Page 187: Garth Oriander; Portraits: Jacqui Henshaw

Photography John Gollings Page 190: John Gollings; Page 191: John Gollings; Page 192: John Gollings, architect Cassandra Fahey; Page 193: John Gollings; Page 194: John Gollings; Page 195: John Gollings; Portrait: Greg Delves **Peter Hyatt**; Page 196: Peter Hyatt; Page 197: Peter Hyatt; Page 198: Peter Hyatt; Page 199: Peter Hyatt; Page 200: Peter Hyatt; Page 201: Peter Hyatt; Portrait: Peter Hyatt **Trevor Mein** Page 202: Trevor Mein; Page 203: Trevor Mein; Page 204: Trevor Mein; Page 205: Trevor Mein; Page 206: Trevor Mein; Portrait: Trevor Mein **Greg Barrett** Page 207: Greg Barrett, from Tutu, Allen & Unwin (1999); Page 208: Greg Barrett; Page 209: Greg Barrett, from Danceshots, Gore & Osment (1993); Page 210: Greg Barrett; Page 211: Greg Barrett; Portrait: Greg Barrett **Daniel MacDougal** Page 213: Daniel MacDougal; Page 214: Daniel MacDougal; Page 215: Daniel MacDougal; Portrait: courtesy of Daniel MacDougal **Andrew Curtis** Page 215: Andrew Curtis; Page 217: Andrew Curtis; Page 218: Andrew Curtis; Page 219: Andrew Curtis; Page 220: Andrew Curtis; Page 221: Andrew Curtis; Portrait: Georgia Curtis

ACKNOWLEDGMENTS

I would like to thank all the people featured in this book for their remarkable work and their conviction to pursue their careers with excellence. Thanks must also go to the many photographers who contributed to this book, bringing the essence of design into our minds.

Thanks also go to Geoff Fitzpatrick, former Victorian president of the Design Institute of Australia, Geoffrey Edwards, director of the Geelong Art Gallery and an honorary curator of glass for the National Gallery of Victoria, and to Helen Quinn, who lectures in the School of Design at Victoria University of Wellington, New Zealand, for suggesting designers for inclusion in this book.

A special thank you to my wife Naomi, and sons James and Timothy, for their support and for allowing a love of design to enter (and sometimes take over) our lives.

Also, a special thankyou to Judith O'Callaghan, senior lecturer in the interior architecture programme at the Univeristy of New South Wales, for her support over the years.

Stephen Crafti

IMAGES is pleased to add *Request.Response.Reaction. The Designers of Australia and New Zealand* to its compendium of design and architecture publications.

We wish to thank all participating designers and firms for their valuable contribution to this publication. In particular, we would like to thank Stephen Crafti for his outstanding work on this project, and acknowledge his support of the design industry in both Australia and New Zealand.

IMAGES is happy to provide contact information for the designers featured in the book. Please visit our website: www.imagespublishinggroup.com and follow the links to Request.Response.Reaction.